*ATP 6-02.40 (FM 6-02.40)

Army Techniques Publication
No. 6-02.40

Headquarters
Department of the Army
Washington, DC, 27 October 2014

TECHNIQUES FOR VISUAL INFORMATION OPERATIONS

Contents

---

*This publication supersedes FM 6-02.40, dated 10 March 2009.

Figures

Tables

Contents

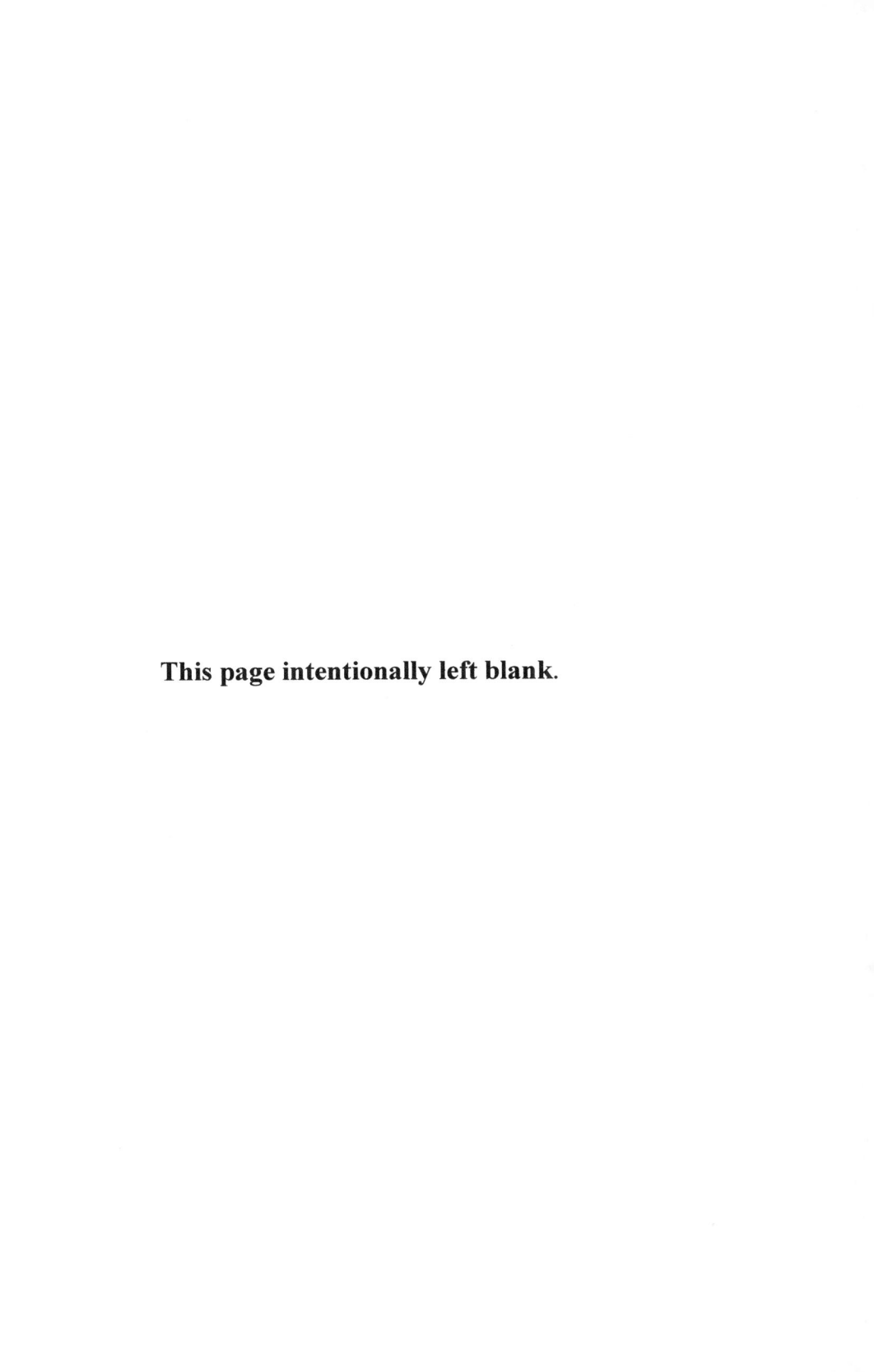

This page intentionally left blank.

Preface

Army Techniques Publication (ATP) 6-02.40, *Techniques for Visual Information Operations*, replaces Field Manual (FM) 6-02.40, *Visual Information Operations*, dated 10 March 2009. ATP 6-02.40 is the primary doctrine publication for visual information operations to support the Army's mission. This manual provides the techniques associated with the components of visual information operations. This manual establishes non-prescriptive ways or methods Signal Soldiers perform missions, functions, and tasks associated with visual information to enable and support the Army's mission at all echelons.

The principal audience for ATP 6-02.40 is commanders, staffs, supervisors, planners, and Signal Soldiers. Commanders, staffs, and subordinates ensure their decisions and actions comply with applicable United States, international, and, in some cases, host nation laws and regulations. Commanders at all levels ensure their Soldiers operate according to the law of war and the rules of engagement (see FM 27-10, *The Law of Land Warfare*).

ATP 6-02.40 uses joint terms where applicable. Selected joint and Army terms and definitions appear in both glossary and the text.

ATP 6-02.40 applies to the Regular Army, Army National Guard of the United States, and United States Army Reserve, unless otherwise stated.

The proponent for this publication is the United States Army Cyber Center of Excellence. The preparing agency is the Cyber Center of Excellence Doctrine Branch, United States Army Cyber Center of Excellence. Send comments and recommendations on a Department of the Army (DA) Form 2028 (Recommended Changes to Publications and Blank Forms) to Commander, United States Army Cyber Center of Excellence and Fort Gordon, ATTN: ATZH-DT (ATP 6-02.40), 506 Chamberlain Avenue, Fort Gordon, GA 30905-5735; or by e-mail to usarmy.gordon.cyber-coe.mbx.gord-fg-doctrine@mail.mil.

Introduction

ATP 6-02.40 expands on the visual information foundations and tenets established in FM 6-02, *Signal Support to Operations*.

Information in ATP 6-02.40 includes roles and responsibilities that enable and support the Army's mission at all echelons. ATP 6-02.40 outlines the Defense Imagery Management Operations Cell and introduces the Joint Imagery Management Operations Cell linked with imagery repository management.

ATP 6-02.40 contains six chapters—

Chapter 1 provides an overview on visual information operations. Discusses the visual information mission, support, and outlines imagery repository management.

Chapter 2 introduces visual information documentation. Defines and addresses visual information documentation including combat camera, operational documentation, technical documentation, and supplemental visual information roles.

Chapter 3 provides an overview of combat camera operations, the associated roles, responsibilities, as well as the organizational structure of the combat camera company. Discusses combat camera support to Army and joint operations.

Chapter 4 provides a description of the various visual information documentation methods and products used to document events and activities.

Chapter 5 outlines the military occupational specialty training and the specialized training associated with visual information operations personnel.

Chapter 6 addresses life cycle sustainment relative to visual information equipment and systems, equipment planning, capability developers, materiel developers, supplies and repair parts, and maintenance.

The glossary lists acronyms and terms with Army, multi-service, or joint definitions, and other selected terms. Where Army and joint definitions are different, *(Army)* follows the term. Terms for which ATP 6-02.40 is the proponent manual (the authority) are marked with an asterisk (*). The proponent manual for other terms is listed in parentheses after the definition.

Chapter 1

Visual Information Overview

This chapter provides an overview on visual information operations. It discusses the visual information mission, support, and outlines imagery repository management. This chapter also outlines how the Defense Imagery Management Operations Center synchronizes and integrates the Department of Defense imagery capabilities as well as centrally manages current and historical visual information.

MISSION

1-1.   The mission of visual information (VI) activities is to capture and provide the President, Office of the Secretary of Defense, Joint Staff, military departments, and Army commanders with VI products and services.

1-2.   Department of Defense Instruction 5040.02 defines VI as information in the form of visual or pictorial representations of person(s), or thing(s), with or without sound. VI includes still photographs, digital still images, motion pictures, analog, digital, and high definition video recordings; hand-generated or computer-generated art and animations that depict real or imaginary person(s) or thing(s); and related captions, overlays, and intellectual control data.

1-3.   The official requirements which VI Soldiers can provide support to may include, but are not limited to, the mission command warfighting function, training, education, logistics, human resources, special operations, information operations (IO), military information support operations (MISO), public affairs, and intelligence to effectively convey accurate intelligence to decisionmakers and supported agencies.

SUPPORT

1-4.   VI support is limited to official events or activities. The priority set for VI support should consider mission, cost effectiveness, quality, and quantity of products and services available. The use of VI products, equipment, or facilities for other than official purposes, such as loaning equipment to local and state governments or nonprofit organizations meeting on government property, is at the discretion of the installation VI manager according to Army Regulation (AR) 700-131.

1-5.   VI support provided by VI and combat camera (COMCAM) personnel enable others to perform the critical mission of providing essential battlefield information to support strategic, operational, and tactical mission objectives. This in turn provides commanders and staffs with the visual tools to support operational planning and decisionmaking requirements. In an age of increasing information density, VI support provides on-scene commanders the required imagery to conduct proper IO, MISO, and civil affairs operations.

1-6.   It is important to understand the distinction between VI activities and other collection activities. Information documented under the auspices of VI activities support a variety of purposes, for example, surveillance, reconnaissance, law enforcement, and medical or intelligence activities. However, when collecting information specifically for one of these purposes, adhere to separate, distinct, policies, regulations, and rules. For further information on excluded activities, see Department of Defense Instruction 5040.02.

DEFENSE IMAGERY MANAGEMENT OPERATIONS CENTER

1-7.   The Defense Imagery Management Operations Center (DIMOC) is *the Department of Defense's (DOD) central VI enterprise level activity for collection, management, storage, and distribution of classified and unclassified strategic, operational, tactical, and joint-interest still and motion imagery, and VI end products and records.*

1-8.   The DIMOC provides worldwide support to the DOD and other United States Government agencies with communications and operational missions with the right imagery in the right place at the right time. The DIMOC conducts integration and coordination with the Defense Media Activity and the Defense Video Imagery Distribution System as depicted in the enterprise imagery product flow. See Figure 1-1.

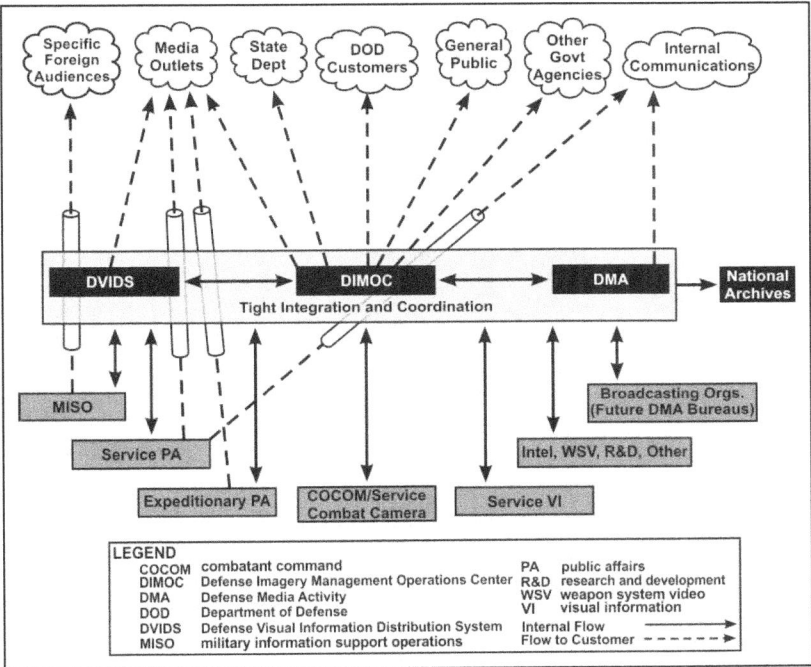

Figure 1-1. Enterprise imagery product flow

1-9.   The Defense Media Activity is the overarching organization for all visual media for the DOD. The Defense Media Activity streamlines DOD media operations through the consolidation of military Service and DOD media components into a single, joint, integrated multimedia communications organization. The Defense Media Activity—

- Provides a variety of information products to the entire DOD family and external audiences through all available media.

- Communicates messages and themes from senior DOD leaders and other leaders in the chain of command, to support and improve quality of life and morale, promote situational awareness, provide timely and immediate force protection information, and sustain readiness.

- Provides United States radio and television news, information, and entertainment programming to the United States military, DOD civilians and contractors, and their families overseas.

- Provides high quality VI products, including COMCAM imagery depicting United States military activities and operations, to the DOD and the American public.

- Provides joint education and training for military and civilian personnel in public affairs, broadcasting, and VI career fields.

1-10. The Defense Video and Imagery Distribution System provide a timely, accurate and reliable connection between the media around the world and the military serving in Iraq, Afghanistan, Kuwait, Qatar and Bahrain. The Defense Video and Imagery Distribution System provides real-time broadcast-quality video, still images and print products as well as immediate interview opportunities with service members, commanders and subject matter experts. The Defense Video and Imagery Distribution System—

- Facilitates interviews with military personnel and subject matter experts engaged in fast-breaking news.
- Links local, national, and international media to military units around the world.
- Enables embedded journalists to transmit broadcast-quality video from the field.
- Fulfills requests for products quickly via satellite, fiber and the internet.
- Provides a variety of newswire services for media.
- Delivers personalized customized subscription e-mail alerts instantly.
- Coordinates holiday greetings, and special events programming involving United States Soldiers, Marines, Sailors, and Airmen around the world.
- Maintains a searchable archive of video, photo, news articles and audio products.
- Makes content available on a variety of external platforms including social media channels, apps and podcasts.

1-11. Distribution of imagery occurs online, via the Defense Imagery Server managed by the DIMOC. The Defense Imagery Server contains still and motion imagery in various formats and resolutions accessible to a worldwide customer base of registered users.

1-12. To accomplish its mission, the DIMOC manages four distinct, but interrelated programs—

- Imagery Operations and Coordination Center. The Imagery Operations and Coordination Center receives, coordinates, and synchronizes classified and unclassified strategic imagery requirements with the Office of the Secretary of Defense, Joint Staff, combatant commands, joint task force, Services, other United States Government departments and agencies, and imagery-producing personnel stationed and deployed around the globe. The program maintains constant visibility of DOD imagery producing personnel, to enable United States Government communications and operational missions. The program ensures that imagery produced for one purpose is available to meet other requirements.
- VI Imagery Management and Distribution Program. The Imagery Management and Distribution Program receives, processes, manages and stores classified and unclassified imagery products created by globally stationed and deployed imagery producing personnel, and provides digital distribution mechanisms that enable the communications and operational missions of the Office of the Secretary of Defense, Joint Staff, combatant commands, joint task force, Services and other United States Government departments and agencies. Imagery products, including still images, raw video, and produced video and multimedia products are received and processed continually by electronic and mechanical means, stored in the digital and physical holdings of the DIMOC, and later offered for further retention in the National Archives.
- VI Order Fulfillment Program. The Order Fulfillment Program delivers imagery products in numerous formats to customers. Imagery products include still images, raw video, produced video, and multimedia products created by DOD imagery producers stationed around the globe. Delivery of imagery products occurs in both physical (prints, videotape, and optical media) and digital formats. Creation or duplication of imagery products takes place on-demand from the digital and physical holdings of the DIMOC.
- VI Customer Service Program. The Customer Service Program receives, manages and distributes customer requests for imagery products and provides customer assistance with DIMOC imagery management and distribution systems.

JOINT IMAGERY MANAGEMENT OPERATIONS CELL

1-13. The Joint Imagery Management Operations Cell provides joint task force commanders critical imagery management and operations support within area of operations. Under this construct, the Joint Imagery Management Operations Cell operates as a deployed DIMOC and provides forward deployed imagery oversight, management, and movement for all imagery to support the joint task force commander and staff. The Joint Imagery Management Operations Cell integrates COMCAM forces and other VI and imagery assets in-theater, establishes mission priorities, and coordinates imagery requirements for the supported staff. Figure 1-2 outlines the Joint Imagery Management Operations Cell. The Joint Imagery Management Operations Cell—

- Helps COMCAM forces in coordinating facilities, transportation, communications, and other logistical support to sustain deployed personnel.
- Plans to employ COMCAM forces during the initial phase of an operation to ensure comprehensive mission documentation. Ensures that COMCAM forces have full access to document the mission, as is reasonably and tactically feasible, during each phase of the operation.
- Ensures that tasking orders and requests for forces identify the operational controlling authority for COMCAM forces in advance of deployment and provide an in-theater point of contact.
- Coordinates with the DIMOC and publish specific guidelines for imagery distribution, clearance, and security classification requirements.

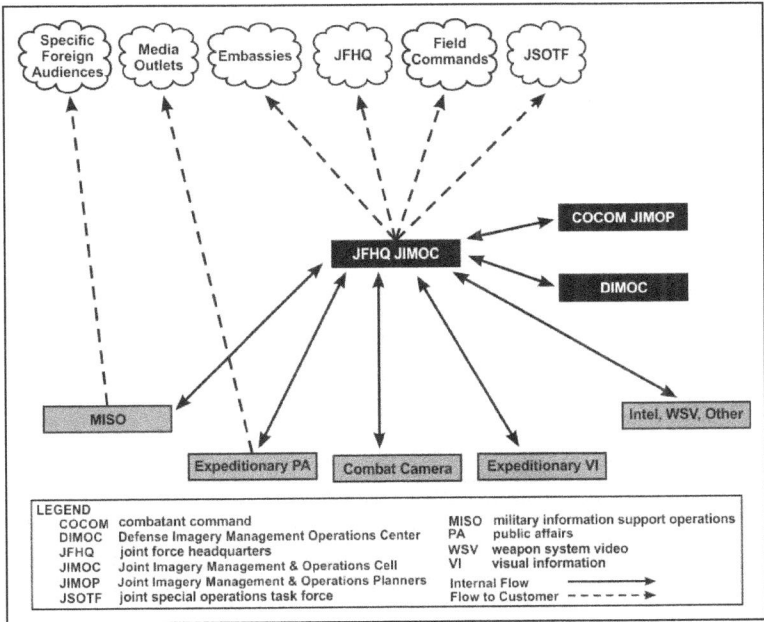

Figure 1-2. Joint imagery management and operations cell

RESPONSIBILITIES

1-14. The Assistant Secretary of Defense (Public Affairs) serves as the Office of the Secretary of Defense Principal Staff Assistant for policies and procedures related to the VI production program.

1-15. The chief information officer/assistant chief of staff, signal (CIO/G-6) Information Infrastructure Integration is responsible for managing the Army's VI activities and coordinating with the Assistant Secretary of Defense (Public Affairs) on VI reporting requirements. The Headquarters Department of the Army (HQDA) CIO/G-6 office—

- Assigns the production identification number to non-local productions.
- Assigns the defense visual information activity number.
- Manages the Content Discovery and Access Log.

1-16. The Installation VI manager—

- Plans, programs, and budgets for all authorized VI requirements in coordination with the installation directorates of plans, training, mobilization, and security.
- Searches the Content Discovery and Access Catalog before completing DD Form 1995 (Visual Information (VI) Production Request and Report).
- Maintains and actively uses the VI Ordering Site to manage and collect metrics for quarterly loading in the Army's Information Technology (IT) Metrics Program.

COMMANDER

1-17. The operational commander is responsible for identifying the requirement for VI support, ensuring there is adequate support for VI assets, and determining collection requirements based on local mission objectives. This includes VI operations in all subordinate or attached commands. Staff officers help commanders in the discharge of their duties.

1-18. The on-scene commander is the releasing authority for all imagery acquired in the theater of operations. The complete cycle from acquisition to receipt by the DIMOC must occur within 24 hours to meet the timely requirements established by the joint force commander. Collected and timely processed imagery creates a viable decisionmaking tool for the leaders at the Office of the Secretary of Defense, the Joint Staff, Defense agencies, Department of State, Department of Homeland Security, combatant commands, public affairs, and military and government agencies.

Operations and Plans Staff Officer

1-19. The operations and plans staff officer at each level of command is responsible for identifying and integrating VI requirements into the operational environment. This integration is critical as it significantly enhances operational decisionmaking.

Visual Information Staff Officer

1-20. The VI staff officer or noncommissioned officer (NCO) at each command level integrates operationally with the component staff and is responsible for helping the signal staff officer in the planning and execution of VI to support the mission. The VI staff officer identifies and integrates VI applications to support operational decisionmaking to prosecute operations at all echelons of command. The VI staff officer defines the capabilities and limitations of VI units and establishes procedures for requesting, validating, and prioritizing VI support. At the theater of operations staff level the COMCAM VI at the assistant chief of staff, signal assumes these duties and responsibilities. At echelons corps and below, the signal staff officer assumes these duties and is advised and assisted by the VI staff officer or NCO.

Combat Camera Team Leader

1-21. The COMCAM team leader produces still and motion imagery to transmit to the DIMOC via portable or fixed long-range transmission systems. The team leader also coordinates the documentation of day and night operations, or aerial documentation with supported units.

Combat Camera Team Member

1-22. COMCAM team members have the following responsibilities—

- Install, operate, and maintain tactical digital media systems.
- Ensure proper image captions on all imagery.
- Perform operator maintenance on tactical digital media equipment, vehicle, and individual equipment.
- Maintain accountability of all on hand equipment.

ACTIVITIES

1-23. VI activities bring together equipment, facilities, and skills essential for generating, preserving, disseminating visual information documentation. VI managers register authorized VI activities and provide information about products and services to the defense imagery website using DD Form 2858 (Visual Information Activity Profile) to create or modify a VI Activity Profile.

1-24. The Enterprise Multimedia Center provides support services such as photography, graphics and design, video and multimedia, as well as sound and presentation. The Army Multimedia and VI Directorate supports the Army and DOD with the following VI services—

- Official photography.
- Digital photography.
- Studio and field television production.
- Video technical services such as duplication.
- Format conversion and editing.
- Graphics presentation design and consulting.
- Exhibit and display services.
- Audiovisual presentation support and consulting.
- Live events management and planning.
- Imagery accessioning.
- Archiving and research services.
- Army pictorial collection management.
- Joint commercial production contracting.
- Acquisition and project management.
- Visual documentation of significant military events in the National Capital Region.
- Visual documentation of national interest events as directed by the President.

VISUAL INFORMATION OPERATIONS

1-25. VI support events and activities that relate to official missions and functions. The use of VI products, equipment, or facilities for other than official purposes, such as loaning equipment to local and state governments or nonprofit organizations meeting on Government property, is at the discretion of the local commander and according to AR 700-131 *Loan, Lease, and Donation of Army Materiel* and AR 735-5 *Property Accountability Policies.*

1-26. Priorities for VI support establish mission, timeliness, cost effectiveness, quality, quantity of products, and services available.

1-27. At the beginning of each quarter, installations VI Managers collect and consolidate data for input into Army's IT Metrics Program. The installation VI Manager coordinates with the Network Enterprise Center office, as the central IT Metrics data collection point, for data deadline information and consolidation of input.

1-28. The services which VI activities offer are outlined in the Command, Control, Communications and Computers Information Management services catalogue and by common levels of support. The specific services of VI activities—

- **Still and Video photography**. Producing, processing, and reproducing still picture film, prints, and slide presentations. This includes electronic still video camera systems.
- **Television**. Producing and reproducing video recordings. This includes briefings, news clips, operational documentation, video reports, and stand-alone video segments, with or without sound.
- **Graphic art**. Designing, creating, and preparing two- and three-dimensional visual products. This includes charts, graphs, posters, visual materials for brochures, covers, television, motion pictures, printed publications, displays, presentations, and exhibits prepared manually, by machine, or by computer.
- **Audio**. Recording, producing, reproducing, and distributing sound to support an activity. This includes recording of briefings, news clips, ambient sound, sound effects, reports, aural amplification, and other studio products.
- **Library**. Loaning and maintaining VI media and equipment. This authorization allows purchase, lease or rental, and accountability of commercial off-the-shelf (COTS) VI productions for local use.
- **Ready access file**. Providing a consolidated electronic source of imagery accessible to official customers.
- **Customer self-help**. Providing self-help support to customers for the production of simple slide presentations, briefing charts, sign-out boards, flyers, or flip charts.
- **Consultation**. Providing customer consultation services to support official requirements for the customer and for professionally developed VI products and services.
- **Content Discovery and Access Catalog**. An online, unrestricted, full-text searchable, standard DOD-wide database containing content description, production, acquisition, inventory, distribution, currency status, archival control, and other data on VI productions and distributive learning course products typically used in military training.
- **Maintenance**. Repairing and servicing organic VI equipment.
- **Broadcast, Video, and Audio services including—**
  - Cable television, operating the command channel(s) provided as part of the cable television franchise agreement.
  - Closed circuit television, providing support to a defined area.
  - Video and Audio, producing audio tapes, providing video streaming and multicast, script preparation, video documentation to support historic and significant events, and duplicating video tapes compact discs and digital video discs to support local VI productions.
- **Media library services**. Authorized VI activities may provide a central library of distributed and local multimedia VI productions and imagery.

VISUAL INFORMATION RECORDS MANAGEMENT

1-29. Control original local or non-local Army multimedia VI productions and VI products with their associated administrative documentation as official records throughout their life cycle and disposal per General Records Schedule 21, Department of Defense Manual 5040.06 *Visual Information (VI)*, and Department of the Army pamphlet (DA Pam) 25-91 *Visual Information Procedures*. For VI housekeeping files, refer to AR 25-400-2 *The Army Records Information Management System (ARIMS)*.

1-30. Activity VI managers maintain a system for numbering individual product items based on Department of Defense Manual 5040.06 requirements. Assign a VI record identification number to still photographs, motion picture footage, video recordings (excluding those assigned a production authorization number or production identification number), and audio recordings, retained for future use. DA Pam 25-91 provides a description of the required VI record identification number elements. Document all VI material retained for future use with a DD Form 2537 (Visual Information Caption Sheet), per procedures outlined in DA Pam 25-91 and AR 25-1 *Army Information Technology*.

1-31. For contractor-produced VI records, the contract specifies the Army's legal title and control of all such VI media and related documentation. Because of their extreme vulnerability to damage, handle VI records according to Department of Defense Manual 5040.06 and associated manuals.

1-32. VI managers maintain continuous custody of permanent or unscheduled VI records before their retirement or submission for accessioning to the DIMOC. If different versions of multimedia VI productions (such as short and long versions, closed-captioned, and foreign language) are prepared, maintain an unaltered copy of each version and forward through the DIMOC for accessioning daily.

Chapter 2

Visual Information Documentation

Visual information documentation provides a visual record of significant Army events and activities and encompasses both tactical and nontactical documentation. This chapter defines and addresses visual information documentation to include combat camera, operational documentation, and technical documentation. This chapter also addresses supplemental visual information roles.

INTRODUCTION

2-1. Department of Defense Instruction 5040.02 defines visual information documentation as motion, still, and audio recording of technical and non-technical events made while occurring, and not usually under, the production control of the recording element. Visual information documentation includes documentation by COMCAM forces.

2-2. Visual information documentation provides a visual record of significant Army events, activities, and encompasses both tactical and non-tactical documentation. Visual information documentation includes COMCAM, operational documentation, technical documentation, and the supplemental roles the Army visual information documentation program provide to the commander. The purpose of the final product dictates the documentation category and provides justification for the initial imagery collection.

2-3. Visual information documentation imagery preserves permanent visual records for historical purposes, such as after action reports, lessons learned, briefings, books, magazine articles, movies, and television programming. This imagery also helps in building unit morale and identity by visually enhancing a unit's history.

2-4. According to AR 25-1, processing visual information documentation requires that each garrison location have a Network Enterprise Center. The garrison Network Enterprise Center designated, as the information manager on an Army post, camp, or station is the single authority for providing common-user IT level support services to include visual information documentation support requirements. Where no post, camp, or station installation configuration exists, the host command or activity coordinates IT services with the respective theater signal command.

COMBAT CAMERA

2-5. COMCAM is a low-density, high-demand force support capability composed of highly trained VI professionals prepared to deploy to the most austere operational environments at a moment's notice. COMCAM provides High Definition digital still imagery and video imagery of ongoing activities and events such as air, sea, and ground actions of armed forces in combat and sustaining operations, catastrophes, natural disasters, training activities, exercises, war games, operations, and peacetime engagements. COMCAM products, called tactical digital media, yield visual imagery, audio, and information upon which commanders and staffs at all levels use to make informed operational decisions.

2-6. When employed, COMCAM provides timely VI to support commanders' objectives and all echelons in a theater of war. COMCAM support packages are adaptive and fully qualified and equipped to document sustained day and night operations. Their modular design facilitates the tailoring of support packages for lesser regional conflicts, small-scale operations and other operations such as peacekeeping and foreign humanitarian relief operations.

2-7. COMCAM requirements should not be confused with public affairs or press pool media requirements. Although used as combat tactical digital media, the primary use of COMCAM products is for public affairs and IO purposes as an operational decisionmaking tool. COMCAM personnel document information and areas of conflict not authorized by media personnel. COMCAM personnel photograph all aspects of an operation or event. Conduct decisions on classification, sensitivity, and clearance for public release through intelligence, operations, and public affairs staff coordination.

TACTICAL DOCUMENTATION

2-8. Tactical documentation is an essential resource that supports unified land operations. Tactical documentation supports the operational and planning requirements of commanders and decisionmakers from the combatant commanders through the President and Secretary of Defense. Tactical documentation is a fundamental tool of commanders and decisionmakers that, when used properly, is an effective combat force multiplier.

2-9. COMCAM teams record tactical digital media to support joint operations, peacetime engagements, limited intervention, peace operations, nontraditional warfare, and major combat operations. COMCAM teams electronically forward imagery, with embedded captions, to the DIMOC for distribution to operational decisionmakers.

NONTACTICAL DOCUMENTATION

2-10. Nontactical (infrastructure) documentation is record documentation of technical, operational, and historical military events as they occur in peacetime. This documentation provides information about people, places, and things as well as Research, Development, Test, and Evaluation.

COMCAM SUPPORT

2-11. COMCAM personnel provide directed imagery capability to support strategic, operational, and planning requirements during wartime operations, worldwide crises, contingencies, joint exercises, and humanitarian operations. The following outlines support methods—

- Operations Support. Visual imagery to support presentations to, and by, higher echelon commands, DOD, the Joint Staff, supporting major commands, unified commands, and the President and Secretary of Defense.
- Support Force Documentation. Still and motion imagery to assess and illustrate support shortfalls, such as environmental equipment, aircraft ramp space, water, fuel, munitions, host nation support, and other support.
- Intelligence Presentation Support. Non-covert still and motion imagery to support intelligence presentations.
- Training Support. Documentation imagery supports the training of forces participating in sustaining operations.
- Historical Record. Imagery supports archival master requirements to depict the significant operational and support efforts of the Department of Defense.
- Site Exploitation. Still and motion imagery to document information, materials, and personnel and their immediate association for the purpose of positive identification, information collection, and support to rule of law.

IMAGERY SUPPORT TO PLANNING

2-12. Imagery support to planning involves the recording of selected or proposed routes into and throughout a particular area. Imagery support to planning occurs in the physical environment in which close combat operations occur. Imagery support to planning allows combat personnel to learn landmarks, building locations, and other visual references to get an accurate visual site image. Motion media can capture these references, as well as noise level, light level, and area traffic in urban areas. Imagery support to planning can also analyze an area before an operation or an employment of forces to the site. Figure 2-1 documents an example of imagery support to planning as Soldiers clear and repair a road.

Figure 2-1. Imagery support to planning

IMAGERY SUPPORT TO BATTLE DAMAGE ASSESSMENT

2-13. Battle damage assessment is the timely and accurate estimate of damage resulting from the application of military force, either lethal or nonlethal, against a predetermined target. Battle damage assessment supports all types of weapon systems (air, ground, naval and Special Forces) across the Services.

2-14. Battle damage assessment is composed of physical damage assessment, functional damage assessment, and target system assessment. This detailed record of battlefield damage against a predetermined target that gives tacticians immediate intelligence, surveillance, and reconnaissance to develop countermeasures to an enemy's weapons and allows logisticians to begin requisitioning appropriate supplies. Still photos or videos provide the necessary intelligence to assess the current situation. Figure 2-2 documents an example of battle damage assessment imagery as a Soldier stands in a crater and assesses damage caused by a bomb dropped during an air strike.

Figure 2-2. Battle damage assessment imagery

GAUGING EFFECTIVENESS IMAGERY

2-15. Gauging effectiveness imagery documents the effectiveness of friendly weapons. Documentation includes how much collateral damage, the enemy's strengths, and weaknesses, and the nature and effectiveness of his countermeasures. The visual imagery obtained through gauging effectiveness imagery accurately communicates information for analysis beyond the capacity of words. Figure 2-3 documents an example of gauging effectiveness imagery.

Figure 2-3. Gauging effectiveness imagery

IMPROVING SITUATIONAL AWARENESS IMAGERY

2-16. Improving situational awareness imagery documents are actual combat conditions in military operations and engagements for the component, theater Army, the President, Secretary of Defense, Chairman of the Joint Chiefs of Staff, and military services staffs for decisionmaking purposes. Figure 2-4 documents an example of improving situational awareness imagery as Soldiers search a boathouse after receiving tips on enemy activity from locals in Iraq.

Figure 2-4. Improving situational awareness imagery

REVIEW IMAGERY

2-17. Review imagery documents initial operation engagements of new weapons and support systems, both friendly and enemy. Review imagery revises friendly tactics or validates doctrine. Commanders can use review imagery to visualize the threat, thereby speeding innovation, and the timely development of counter-tactics, and revised doctrine. Figure 2-5 documents an example of review imagery.

Figure 2-5. Review imagery

OPERATIONAL DOCUMENTATION

2-18. Operational documentation activities provide information about people, places, and things. Operational documentation is general-purpose documentation normally done in peacetime. Most VI activities at installations perform operational documentation as a major part of their mission. Common support activities provide operational documentation to all units, staffs, agencies, and organizations that require VI support to accomplish their missions. Examples of operational documentation are public affairs, command information, construction and renovation projects, safety office reports, fire department reports, personnel and community affairs projects, and photographs. Some operational documentation material has only temporary value, and other material has lasting historical importance.

READINESS POSTURE IMAGERY

2-19. Readiness posture imagery displays a unit's readiness. Readiness posture imagery uses still photos or videos to provide the necessary information to the Commander about the readiness posture of the unit. Figure 2-6 documents an example of readiness posture imagery as Soldiers prepare for a Joint Readiness Training Exercise rotation.

Figure 2-6. Readiness posture imagery

SIGNIFICANT OPERATIONS IMAGERY

2-20. Significant operations imagery documents situations and supports public or community affairs programs. Examples are images of operations, exercises, or maneuvers captured for historical or public affairs purposes. Figure 2-7 documents an example of significant operations imagery as a United States Army unit provides food and humanitarian supplies to an Iraqi police officer in Iraq during a food distribution mission.

Figure 2-7. Significant operations imagery

SIGNIFICANT PROGRAMS AND PROJECTS IMAGERY

2-21. Significant programs and projects imagery documents programs and projects that impact national or Army policy. These images track progress, provide status, or document the accomplishment of significant milestones. Figure 2-8 documents the ribbon cutting for the grand opening of the South Park Post Office on Kandahar Airfield, Afghanistan.

Figure 2-8. Significant programs and projects imagery

CIVIL MILITARY INVOLVEMENT IMAGERY

2-22. Civil military involvement imagery documents operating conditions, chronicling Army efforts and participation in disaster relief, civil disturbances, and environmental protection. Civil military involvement imagery contributes to public affairs and community relations programs to keep the public abreast of developments. The still and video imagery transcends the language barrier and allows better cooperation between the representatives of the military and local citizens, both American and foreign. Figure 2-9 documents an example of civil military involvement imagery as Soldiers provide critical care to citizens of a disaster.

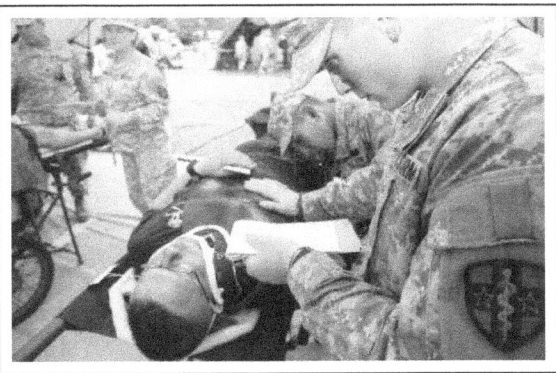

Figure 2-9. Civil military involvement imagery

CONSTRUCTION IMAGERY

2-23. Construction imagery documents construction of systems, facilities, and installations. Construction imagery demonstrates project progress and provides information for future operations, after action reviews, and lessons learned. Figure 2-10 documents an example of construction imagery.

Figure 2-10. Construction imagery

SIGNIFICANT MILITARY EVENTS IMAGERY

2-24. Significant military events imagery provides a visual historical record of base closures and realignments; activation and deactivation, deployment, or a change of command of a division or larger unit; and general officer promotions. Figure 2-11 documents an example of significant military event imagery.

Figure 2-11. Significant military event imagery

MILITARY LIFE IMAGERY

2-25. Military life imagery documents Soldiers at work, physical training, new equipment usage, and quality of life. Figure 2-12 documents an example of military life imagery.

Figure 2-12. Military life imagery

TECHNICAL DOCUMENTATION

2-26. Technical documentation is documentation of an actual event taken to evaluate it. Technical documentation contributes to the study of human or mechanical factors, procedures, and processes in the fields of medicine, science, logistics, intelligence, investigations, and armament delivery. Technical documentation has the potential to become permanent record material. Figure 2-13 documents a Stryker mobile gun system firing high explosive anti-tank rounds at targets on a digital multipurpose training range.

Figure 2-13. Evaluation imagery

2-27. VI activities at proving grounds, missile ranges, hospitals, research centers, and similar installations primarily engage in technical documentation, and perform some operational documentation. Timely identification and preservation of record material is important for all VI activities, especially those concerning technical documentation.

SUPPLEMENTAL VISUAL INFORMATION ROLES

2-28. In addition to preserving permanent visual records for historical purposes, visual information documentation supports supplemental VI roles. The following paragraphs address the visual information documentation that supports supplemental VI roles.

LEGAL DOCUMENTATION IMAGERY

2-29. Legal documentation imagery provides hard visual evidence in the prosecution or defense of law of war issues or to complete investigators' accident or incident investigations. Legal documentation imagery also provides photographic proof of damage supporting United States government property damage claims by or against foreign governments. Figure 2-14 documents an example of legal documentation imagery.

Figure 2-14. Legal documentation imagery

MILITARY INFORMATION SUPPORT OPERATIONS IMAGERY

2-30. MISO are a vital part of the broad range of United States political, military, economic and ideological activities used by the United States Government to secure national objectives. MISO are planned operations to convey selected information and indicators to foreign audiences to influence their emotions, motives, objective reasoning, and ultimately the behavior of foreign governments, organizations, groups, and individuals in a manner favorable to the United States policy and national objectives.

SIMULATION IMAGERY

2-31. Simulations imagery recreates events through technology. Imagery of actual operations enables commanders in imparting the highest degree of realism to simulation by including actual scenes from operations to aide in the detailed recreation of events. Simulation imagery enables commanders to use computers and advanced software packages to recreate entire operational engagements to execute operations with pinpoint accuracy. During simulations operations, various video outputs ranging from desktops to projection screens display imagery, which enhances simulation operations and enables interactive simulations and potentially elevates the technology from a training tool to an intelligence and mission command tool. Figure 2-15 documents a graphical representation of simulated imagery.

Figure 2-15. Simulation imagery

Chapter 3

Combat Camera Operations

This chapter provides an overview of combat camera operations, the associated roles, responsibilities, as well as the organizational structure of the combat camera company. This chapter also discusses combat camera support to Army and Joint operations.

COMBAT CAMERA OVERVIEW

3-1. The COMCAM forces provide the Office of the Secretary of Defense, Chairman of the Joint Chiefs of Staff, the military departments, combatant commands, and the joint task force with a directed imagery capability to support operational and planning requirements through the full range of military operations.

3-2. The COMCAM company supports land, airborne, airmobile, and sea operations. When deployed as a whole, the company supports Soldiers at all echelons across the range of military operations. The company can deploy on short notice to support any level of combat force projection down to the brigade combat team. The COMCAM company also operates in a joint operational environment supporting a Joint COMCAM organization.

3-3. The trained and equipped COMCAM company operates under all weather and lighting conditions with both conventional and special operations units. The COMCAM company maintains airborne qualified Service Members who perform other advanced tactical training including air assault, combat lifesaver, and advanced marksmanship techniques and provides the following capabilities—

- Tactical digital media.
- Editing capabilities.
- Transmission of VI products for conventional, non-conventional, and airborne operations.
- High definition camera equipment (this allows for one person to shoot still and video images which is an important consideration for small-unit planning, such as special operations, ranger, and pathfinder operations).
- Graphic design.

3-4. Whether documenting training exercises for critique or capturing images of a humanitarian relief effort, COMCAM must be able to tell a complete story for the audience.

COMBAT CAMERA SUPPORT TO INFORMATION OPERATIONS

3-5. COMCAM is a supporting capability of IO. Employment of COMCAM assets and capabilities occurs to achieve desired effects in the physical, informational, and cognitive dimensions of the information environment. COMCAM documentation synchronized with public information and coordinated by IO enables successful conduct of operations. The integration of COMCAM documentation into IO maximizes commanders and staffs at all levels ability to make informed operational decisions, and enable larger influence on larger audiences during operations.

MISSION COMMAND

3-6. The Joint Chiefs of Staff and the United States Army Forces Command (FORSCOM) generate mission taskings for Army COMCAM teams. The CIO/G-6 and FORSCOM assistant chief of staff, operations are responsible for ensuring that all contingency and war plans include COMCAM requirements in their operation annexes.

3-7. Commanders involved in wartime operations, worldwide crises, contingencies, joint exercises, and other events involving DOD components having significant national interest plan for, task, sustain, and employ COMCAM forces.

3-8. COMCAM teams when deployed work in a joint environment as members of the joint COMCAM team. The joint operational mission command is at the joint force level through the information operations division of the operations directorate of a joint staff. The information operations division of the operations directorate of a joint staff is responsible for COMCAM activities. FORSCOM retains administrative control of COMCAM teams while the joint force commander maintains operational control exercised through the joint COMCAM team.

ROLE OF THE ARMY COMPONENT HEADQUARTERS AND STAFF

3-9. FORSCOM is responsible for COMCAM mission requests and taskings and requirements for COMCAM support to FORSCOM. FORSCOM ensures that subordinate commands integrate tactical COMCAM support requirements into their operations plans.

3-10. The CIO/G-6, Army VI Management Office serves as the functional proponent for COMCAM.

3-11. The assistant chief of staff plans ensure that COMCAM documentation support is included in Army operational planning documents for operations plans, contingency plans, and training exercises.

3-12. The United States Army Network Enterprise Technology Command—

- Organize and operate Army deployable COMCAM teams through the two COMCAM units, one each in the Regular Army and Army Reserve. Teams provide tactical digital media of operational contingencies, exercises, joint operations, and relief activities in response to major disasters and other peacetime engagements.
- Provide worldwide COMCAM documentation support for Army, joint exercises and joint service military operations, contingencies, emergencies, and other peacetime engagements. This includes participation in development and maintenance of appropriate war plans.

3-13. The Commanding General, United States Army Training and Doctrine Command in concert with the Network Enterprise Command, develops capability and materiel development plans and concepts for COMCAM organizations and systems. The Training and Doctrine Command prepares the table of organization and equipment in the force structure for COMCAM organizations and prepares stated objectives (ends) for COMCAM organizations and systems.

3-14. Commanders of Army components of unified, subunified, and specified commands integrate tactical COMCAM support requirements into operational plans for contingencies and national disasters in accordance with the Joint Operations Planning and Execution System.

COMCAM COMPANY OPERATIONS

3-15. The COMCAM company is a force multiplier for all elements of Army operations. COMCAM personnel are also low-density, high profile, and rapidly deployable. The COMCAM company deploys as teams. The COMCAM teams' response capacities are equal to the forces they deploy with, and they train with those units when possible. Elements of the company support airborne operations for forced entry and rapid deployment missions. Typical COMCAM support to the division sections include the following—

- Assistant chief of staff, personnel section for historical, legal, safety information.
- Assistant chief of staff, intelligence section for counter intelligence, terrain analysis, targeting, situational awareness, and intelligence missions.
- Assistant chief of staff, operations section for operational assessment, reconnaissance, decisionmaking, incident verification, and IO.
- Assistant chief of staff, sustainment section for equipment use, support conditions, sustainment infrastructure.
- Assistant chief of staff, plans section for contingency, operational, and deception planning.
- Assistant chief of staff, signal section for signal site evaluation, systems integration.

- Assistant chief of staff, information operations section for cyber security, physical security, physical attack, counters intelligence, COMCAM, and concept development.
- Assistant chief of staff, resource management section for resource management, manpower, personnel and equipment authorizations, government purchase card and government travel charge card programs.
- Assistant chief of staff, civil affairs operations section for civil support, maneuver coordination, Unified Land Operations.

SUPPORT REQUIREMENTS

3-16. Corps COMCAM teams are attached to corps units and provide tactical digital media from the corps headquarters down to battalion level. COMCAM teams respond as an integral part of the information element of combat power and communication synchronization.

3-17. At the theater level, the COMCAM company is attached to the theater Army. The company supports theater and corps sized elements, while working directly for the theater and corps operations directorate of a joint staff or assistant chief of staff, operations IO—

- The theater Army element provides support and services associated with warfighting functions.
- Provides tactical digital media transmission on data-capable communications lines across the theater of operations and back to the sustaining base.
- The theater Army provides communications-electronics maintenance support to the COMCAM company.

3-18. At the corps and division levels, the COMCAM element is under operation control of the headquarters—

- The platoon headquarters is co-located with the appropriate corps or division assistant chief of staff, operations under the IO.
- The associated Army element provides food service, health, legal, religious, resource management, human resources, administrative services, supply, supplemental air transportation, and support for transmission of VI on data-capable communications lines across the corps or division and to the next higher headquarters.
- The corresponding signal command provides communications-electronics maintenance support.

3-19. COMCAM imagery supports the military commander's operation themes and messages, enhances situational awareness, and is a historical operations record. COMCAM provides historical documentation of ongoing military operations and support communication synchronization objectives by integrating and synchronizing the acquisition and distribution of still and video imagery. Table 3-1 on page 3-4, provides examples of typical COMCAM supported mission areas.

Table 3-1. Examples of combat camera mission support

Training Support	Operational Assessment	Recovery
Battle Damage Assessment	Special Operations	Countering Weapons of Mass Destruction
Military Information Support Operations	Civil Affairs	Develop Actionable Information
Information Operations	Disaster Relief	Countering Weapons of Mass Destruction
Homeland Security	Force Protection	Counterinsurgency
Counterterrorism	Civil-Military Operations	Offense Stability Operations
Domestic Operations	Peace Operations	Defense Stability Operations
Counterdrug Operations	Foreign Humanitarian Assistance	Homeland Defense
Media Relations	Website Content	Investigation Support (Legal Documentation)
Crisis Management	Command Information	Homeland Defense
News Releases	Press Briefings	Develop Evidentiary Documentation
Site Exploitation	Attack the Network	Rule of Law

3-20. To support austere environments, COMCAM elements can deploy with limited low data rate satellite transmission capability. Most COMCAM imagery is transmitted using theater-deployed or fixed commercial communications. The DIMOC is not responsible for clearing imagery for public release; this function is the responsibility of the on-scene commander. The DIMOC can receive imagery classified up to the SECRET level via electronic means on the SECRET Internet Protocol Router Network. Until cleared for public release, forward uncleared imagery to the DIMOC as *For Official Use Only*.

3-21. The DIMOC serves as the DOD central reception and distribution point for joint interest imagery. The DIMOC has the primary mission of distributing operational imagery to the Joint Staff for the daily Joint Chiefs of Staff briefing. The DIMOC employs a secure 16 hours per day, five days per week imagery operation and coordination center that supports the operational planning, timely imagery acquisition, and integration of VI activities across multiple echelons. The imagery operation and coordination center facilitates the handling of uncleared and classified imagery.

3-22. A designated representative, working under the authority of the on-scene commander, typically accomplishes a security review. The goal of the security review is to protect classified material and prevent inadvertent disclosure. Mark unclassified imagery deemed sensitive in nature as "For Official Use Only, Not for Release." If an image contains classified information, the caption should specify what exactly is classified. In some cases, the text of a caption may be the only classified part of an image file. The authority that has classified an image must be listed in the caption, along with that person's title, unit name, and contact information (in case of declassification review).

3-23. The local public affairs representative or other designated representative at the lowest possible level reviews all unclassified imagery from COMCAM Soldiers or non-COMCAM soldiers who use their own personal cameras for their personal use but in an operational environment, for possible public release, including social media, unless otherwise directed by public affairs guidance or higher authority. The local public affairs representative or other designated representative is also responsible for identifying COMCAM imagery as, *Not Cleared for Public Release* at any level in the review process, to prevent inadvertent release of *Unclassified, but Sensitive* imagery to the public.

3-24. Reviewing and clearing imagery at the lowest possible level expedites the movement of imagery to customers who have an immediate need for unclassified published imagery. Public release procedures define applicable operations plans, operations orders, and applicable supporting annexes.

STRUCTURE

3-25. The modular standardized design of the COMCAM company facilitates meeting their mission requirements at the tactical level of operations more accurately reflect its emerging role in strategic and tactical requirements. Figure 3-1 depicts the COMCAM company organizational structure.

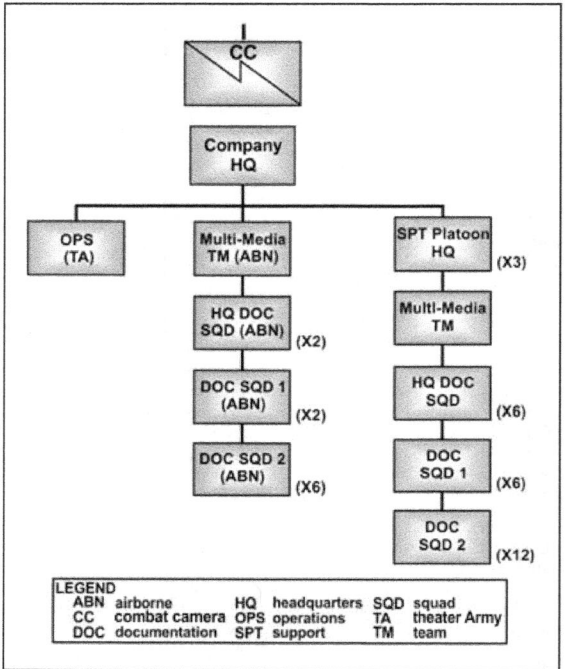

Figure 3-1. Combat camera company organizational structure

3-26. The COMCAM company deploys as teams. The structure and training for COMCAM units allows them to tailor missions to scalable requirements that include airborne and small-unit operations as depicted in Figure 3-2.

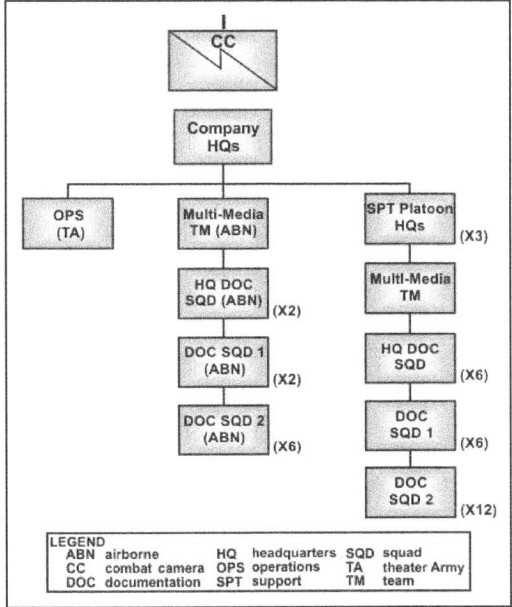

Figure 3-2. Combat camera company (Airborne) organizational structure

Company Headquarters

3-27. The company headquarters provides mission command and supervision of operations and activities to ensure execution of their Joint, Unified, and United States Army visual information documentation missions. The company headquarters (refer to Table 3-2) provides limited administrative and logistical support for all assigned personnel, including procuring the operational, logistical, and information services required to accomplish the mission. The company headquarters ensures the integration of risk management at all subordinate echelons. The commander sets risk approval authority elements. For detailed risk management integration information, see ATP 5-19 *Risk Management*.

Table 3-2. Company headquarters

Grade	Military Occupational Specialty	Position
O-4	25A00	Commander
E-8	25Z50	First Sergeant
E-6	92Y30	Supply Sergeant
E-5	74D20	Chemical, Biological, Radiological, and Nuclear Noncommissioned Officer
E-5	91B20	Wheeled Vehicle Mechanic
E-4	42A10	Human Resources Specialist
E-4	91B10	Wheeled Vehicle Mechanic
E-4	91C10	Utilities Equipment Repairer

Table 3-2. Company headquarters *(continued)*

Grade	Military Occupational Specialty	Position
E-4	92Y10	Supply Specialist
E-3	91B10	Wheeled Vehicle Mechanic

Support Platoon

3-28. The support platoon (refer to Table 3-3) provides VI support for ground, air assault and amphibious missions. The COMCAM company consists of three support platoons. Each support platoon is comprised of—

- A platoon headquarters, which provides command, control, supervision, and staff planning for the Platoon in the performance of support missions.
- A multimedia team that provides still and video editing for a finished product at division, corps, and theater through the utilization of a Still Photography Editing and Processing System and a Motion Video Editing System. The multimedia team also provides tailored still and motion media products, graphics products, narration support, video reports, presentation and visual imagery to support operational headquarters, video and still editing, and archive production of COMCAM documentation products.
- Two headquarters documentation squads that provide mission command for two documentation teams.
- Two documentation teams that provide COMCAM VI support to operations and other assigned mission support. The documentation teams provide conventional still, digital still and video products, and rough editing to the on-site customer.

Table 3-3. Support platoon

Grade	Military Occupational Specialty	Position
O-2	25A00	Platoon Leader
E-7	25Z40	Platoon Sergeant
E-7	25Z40	Visual Information Imagery Management Chief
E-6	25V30	Squad Leader
E-5	25V20	Combat Documentation Production Specialist
E-4	25M10	Tactical Multimedia Specialist
E-4	25R10	Visual Information Equipment Operator-Maintainer
E-4	25V10	Combat Documentation Production Specialist
E-3	25M10	Multimedia Illustrator
E-3	25V10	Combat Documentation Production Specialist
E-3	25V10	Combat Documentation Production Specialist

Theater Operations Section

3-29. The theater operations section (refer to Table 3-4, page 3-8) provides planning, coordination and supervision of operations of all Theater, Corps, and Division level COMCAM documentation support missions. The theater operations section ensures the execution of COMCAM visual documentation for Joint, Unified, and United States Army operations by assigned platoons. The theater operations section exercises direct control over the documentation and multimedia sections of the company assigned to it.

Table 3-4. Theater operations section

Grade	Military Occupational Specialty	Position
O-3	25A00	Operations Officer
E-8	25Z50	Visual Information Liaison Noncommissioned Officer

COMMUNICATIONS

3-30. The theater Army COMCAM company passes *classified* and *unclassified* orders, imagery, data, and command and operational information at the theater, corps, and division levels over internet protocol networks. COMCAM elements operate an internal frequency modulation network for mission command and operate within the supported unit's network. The company employs organic communications equipment to support this requirement.

3-31. The primary communications capability employed by the COMCAM company is the single channel ground and airborne radio system. The COMCAM company also use telephones for staff coordination. In an austere environment, COMCAM elements can deploy with limited stand-alone transmission capability via portable low data rate satellite transmission systems. Theater deployed or fixed communication such as the Non-Secure Internet Protocol Router Network and the SECRET Internet Protocol Router Network enable the transport of most COMCAM still and video imagery.

3-32. The broadband global area network also supports COMCAM company communication requirements. The broadband global area network supports internet protocol technology as well as traditional circuit-switched voice and data. There are wide varieties of small user terminals available that provide performance options to suit different operational needs. The broadband global area network provides VI Soldiers the capability to communicate from nearly anywhere in the world.

3-33. The broadband global area network provides simultaneous voice and broadband data on a global basis. It provides secure reachback and in-theater of operations interoperability through a single, portable terminal compatible with both circuit-switched and internet protocol based cryptographic devices. The broadband global area network enables internet protocol based data connectivity for e-mail, internet, and virtual private network access, while supporting simultaneous voice and Integrated Services Digital Network. The broadband global area network uses International Maritime Satellite for mobile broadband services. The broadband global area network supports the latest internet protocol based services, as well as traditional circuit-switched voice and data, integrating seamlessly with existing networks. The broadband global area network provides Soldiers the capability to select guaranteed data rates on-demand, to support a range of video-based applications. The broadband global area network is equipped with high and low-gain antennas and is compatible with current and legacy systems.

THEATER COMBAT CAMERA VISUAL INFORMATION OFFICER

3-34. The COMCAM company commander or platoon leader serves as the theater COMCAM VI officer at the assistant chief of staff, for the signal command (theater) at the Army Service component command (ASCC). The theater COMCAM VI officer responsibilities include—

- Advising and providing recommendations to the commander and the assistant chief of staff, operations on the capabilities, limitations, and employment of COMCAM assets to support mission objectives.
- Making recommendations on the capabilities, limitations, and employment of COMCAM assets to support the mission objectives.
- Planning and recommending COMCAM missions, and monitoring execution of decisions.
- Preparing, updating, and maintaining COMCAM annexes to plans and orders.
- Processing, analyzing, and disseminating COMCAM information, including submitting COMCAM products and information to the appropriate staff element.
- Conducting staff coordination with the command, other staff officers, and sections at the higher, lower, adjacent, and supporting echelons of command and corresponding joint staff elements.

JOINT COMBAT CAMERA OPERATIONS

3-35. COMCAM empowers the joint force commander by capturing, processing, and distributing classified and unclassified still and motion imagery to support Unified Land Operations. Imagery captured during COMCAM operations ensures an accurate record of ongoing operations, and is vital to communication missions. Each military Service has dedicated COMCAM units specially trained and equipped to support combat forces in any environment. All COMCAM Soldiers must have received advanced field training and weapons qualifications. All personnel who require access to information systems processing classified defense information to fulfill their duties possess a security clearance based on the appropriate personnel security investigation per Department of Defense Instruction 5200.02, *DOD Personnel Security Program.*

3-36. Army COMCAM teams are tasked to participate in DOD joint exercises along with COMCAM teams from other services. Only the Chairman of the Joint Chiefs of Staff and combatant commanders has the authority to task joint service COMCAM teams. Tasking is normally component-specific (Army COMCAM is tasked to document Army activities); however in a joint environment, joint COMCAM forces can be formed to document all aspects of an operation.

3-37. Joint COMCAM support is an operational mission of the information operations division of the operations directorate of a joint staff. Appendix 11 to Annex C of the operations plan addresses COMCAM deliberate plans. Other functions may cross-reference COMCAM support in their respective annexes.

3-38. The information operations division of the operations directorate of a joint staff and the Joint Staff, Deputy Director for Global Operations (J-39) is responsible for COMCAM activities. The J-39 generates COMCAM mission assignments and receives assignments from both higher authority and from within the joint force. The J-39 establishes priorities and coordinates support for COMCAM missions with requesting commanders within the joint force. The lead officer in charge of the joint COMCAM team reports directly to the J-39 to integrate COMCAM into the joint force major operations plan and serves as the senior COMCAM advisor of the information operations division of the operations directorate of a joint staff. The lead officer in charge of the joint COMCAM team coordinates COMCAM requirements outside the purview of COMCAM team through the J-39. Under guidance of the J-39, the joint COMCAM team lead is responsible for receiving, prioritizing, directing, and coordinating operational assignments for the deployed COMCAM teams.

3-39. In coordination with the information operations division of the operations directorate of a joint staff and J-39, the joint COMCAM team lead develops a documentation plan for both the Joint COMCAM team and Service COMCAM assets. The joint COMCAM team lead directs COMCAM team documentation taskings. Components retain administrative control for their COMCAM forces within the joint force. COMCAM routinely receives documentation requests from other functional areas through the information operations division of the operations directorate of a joint staff via the J-39. The joint COMCAM team lead advises the various staff elements on effective application of COMCAM assets in developing requirements.

3-40. Joint COMCAM teams acquire still and motion imagery via digital format. Based on the requirement, the number of teams and composition needed to document a mission varies. The teams attach to the unit that it documents and receives logistically support from that unit. Frequently, COMCAM teams move to cover multiple units in a theater of operations and tactical control may transfer multiple times at the discretion of the joint force commander through the joint COMCAM team lead. Field commanders are encouraged to use COMCAM teams for operational imagery requirements. The following require prioritization of mission tasking to ensure COMCAM availability—

- Emergent imagery requirements.
- Documentation of capture of persons of interest.
- Destruction of equipment, or events of high visibility.

This page intentionally left blank.

Chapter 4

Documentation Methods and Products

This chapter describes the various visual information documentation methods and products used to document events and activities.

DOCUMENTATION METHODS

4-1. Documentation methods depend on the type of documentation, the environment in which the documentation takes place and the support available to personnel documenting the event. COMCAM personnel use motion media, still photography, and audio recording to document events. Motion media and still photography consists of three tiers—

- Tier 1 High end production.
- Tier 2 Professional COMCAM.
- Tier 3 Consumer.

MEDIA FORMATS

4-2. Transmitting and archiving visual information documentation require conversion of the media into a format that reduces transmission and archive capacity. Visual information documentation consists of the following media formats—

- **Motion Standard Definition and Motion High Definition Video.** Motion standard definition and motion high definition video use H.264 compression. H.264 also known as Moving Pictures Experts Group-4 is an industry standard for video compression. H.264 compression converts digital video into a format that takes up less capacity when the video is stored or transmitted.
- **Still Imagery and Graphics.** Still imagery and graphics use Joint Photographic Experts Group-12 compression.
- **Audio.** Audio uses pulse code modulation in the form of waveform audio file format compression and Audio Interchange File Format compression.

Motion Media

4-3. Motion media is visual information documentation of activities or operations as they occur, complemented by audio documentation. Motion media technology can accommodate daytime, nighttime, and limited visibility operations. Table 4-1 on page 4-2, provides examples of motion media capture and transmission formats.

Table 4-1. Motion media capture and transmission formats

Environment	Tier 1 High end production	Tier 2 Professional combat camera and public affairs	Tier 3 Consumer
Capture formats			
Movie	35 millimeter Film RedCam		IPhone Camera Digital and Tape CamCorders 720p
Broadcast	1080 Progressive (p) 1080 Interlaced (i)	1080p 1080i 720p 720i	
Documentation	1080p 1080i	1080p 1080i 720p 720i	IPhone Cam Digital and Tape Camcorders 720p
Production		1080p 1080i 720p 720i	
Transmission formats			
Movie	Proxy Sneakernet Hard Drives		
Production	Proxy Sneakernet Hard Drives	1080i Hard drive Tape Master	
Broadcast	Society of Motion Picture and Television Engineers 274M-2003	Fast Fourier Transform 720p 1080i Hard drive Tape Master	Upload You Tube and Vimeo
Documentation	Society of Motion Picture and Television Engineers 274M-2003	Fast Fourier Transform 720p	Upload You Tube and Vimeo
These are preferred specifications. Submit the best available quality possible, based on the transmission capability.			

4-4.   Figure 4-1 documents an example of motion media.

Figure 4-1. Motion media

Still Photography

4-5. Still photography involves producing, processing, and reproducing still picture films, prints, and slides. These images can be captured using film or digital camera photography, motion picture, or video photography.

Digital Still Photography

4-6. Digital still photography cameras capture images electronically. The images are stored on an internal camera memory or removable memory devices transfer information systems for viewing and printing immediately. Some cameras are equipped with night vision devices that permit the cameras to be used during darkness or other limited light conditions.

4-7. Digital still photography cameras can capture images such as terrain features, tactical deployments, operational information, and tactical operations taken directly from the operational environment. Table 4-2 on page 4-4, provides examples of still photography capture and transmission formats.

Table 4-2. Still photography capture and transmission formats

Environment	Tier 1 High end production		Tier 2 Professional combat camera and public affairs		Tier 3 Consumer
Capture formats					
Publication	Raw		Raw		Various
Documentation	Raw and JPEG 12		Raw and JPEG 12		Various
Base and Post	JPEG 12		JPEG 12		Various
Individual	JPEG 12		JPEG 12		Various
Transmission formats					
Publication	JPEG 12		JPEG 12		JPEG 12
Documentation	JPEG 12		JPEG 12		JPEG 12
Base and Post	JPEG 12		JPEG 12		JPEG 12
Individual	JPEG 12		JPEG 12		JPEG 12
Graphics formats					
Publication	InDesign Pagemaker Photoshop	Layered	InDesign Pagemaker Photoshop	Layered	Various
Documentation	InDesign Pagemaker Photoshop	Layered	InDesign Pagemaker Photoshop	Layered	Various
Base and Post	InDesign Pagemaker Photoshop	Layered	InDesign Pagemaker Photoshop	Layered	Various
Scanned Graphic	JPEG 12	Flat	JPEG 12	Flat	Various

Legend:
JPEG Joint Photographic Experts Group

4-8.   Figure 4-2 documents an example of still photography.

Figure 4-2. Still photography

Audio

4-9. Audio documentation records, stores, and reproduces sound by using audio recording systems integrated with digital recorders or by using portable microphones and audio recorders. Various storage technologies and audio file formats record and store audio documentation. Table 4-3 depicts the archival format specifications for media agreed upon by the DIMOC and National Archives and Records Administration Special Media Services.

Table 4-3. Archival formats specifications

Media type	Specifications
Motion Standard Definition	
Format	H.264
Resolution	640x480
Color Bit Rate	10
Frames	10 frames per second
Data Rate	1.5 megabits per second
Compression Ratio	83:1
Sampling	4:2:2
Motion High Definition	
Format	H.264
Resolution	1280x720
Color Bit Rate	12
Frames	29.97 frames per second
Data Rate	6 megabits per second
Compression Ratio	180:1
Sampling	4:2:2
Still Imagery	
Format	Joint Photographic Experts Group-12 (uncompressed) Optimized Baseline
Magazine	
Format	Portable Document Format-Archive Optical Character Recognition, Flattened
Graphic	
Format	Joint Photographic Experts Group-12 (uncompressed) Optimized Baseline
Audio	
Format	Pulse Code Modulation (Waveform Audio File Format and Audio Interchange File Format)
Sampling	48 kilohertz

VISUAL INFORMATION PRODUCTION AND DISTRIBUTION

4-10. VI production provides official organizational video communications created at any level within the DOD. VI productions are—

- Life-cycle-managed and produced by authorized VI activities.
- Issued a defense visual information activity number or contracted with approval at the DOD component headquarters level.
- Prioritized through internal resources.
- Used for recording, producing, reproducing, processing, broadcasting, editing, distributing, exhibiting, and storing VI products.

4-11. The life cycle of a VI production begins when the functional proponent plans and programs resources to establish and justify the requirement in the ASCC annual production and distribution program. A VI production is the combining or arranging any separate audio or visual product(s) in continuity, in a self-contained, complete presentation that develop according to a plan or script for conveying information to, or communicating with, an audience.

4-12. Used collectively, VI production refers to the functions of procurement, production, or adoption from all sources, including in-house or contract production, commercial off the shelf acquisition, or adoption from another DOD component or federal agency.

4-13. VI managers ensure that the responsible functional proponent that manages the resources for the area requiring support validates each requirement for production at each appropriate level (installation, ASCC or field operating agency, HQDA). The functional proponent or the designated representative evaluates and obtains funding to support the production, objective, and legitimacy of the program.

4-14. All VI managers ensure that the Army does not produce or support productions or other products used to influence pending legislation or to promote the status of any commercial industry. Productions dealing with history and art must educate, train, and inform, not promote the DOD organizational role. VI productions will not contain material that—

- Portrays military and DOD personnel in unfavorable or undignified circumstances unless it is essential to the message conveyed.
- Implies endorsement of commercial products or services by introducing trademarks, labels, distinctive packaging, or reference to trade or brand names in the narration, dialogue, or titles.
- Promotes an individual, activity, or organization, or provides forums for opinions on broad subjects without reference to specific programs.
- Is inaccurate or incompatible with DOD policies or doctrine.
- Discriminates or appears to discriminate against individuals based on sex, race, creed, nationality, age, religion, or national origin.

4-15. VI managers do not reproduce any DOD or Army-wide production completely or in part without prior approval of the ASCC or the field operating agency VI manager, DIMOC, and Army VI Management Office. VI managers ensure that production records meet legal requirements before approval.

4-16. VI managers do not reproduce purchased, rented, or adopted commercial products authorized for exhibition in their original distribution format. Federal copyright laws and specific procurement conditions govern each individual production title. The Army may specify internal distribution restrictions for any of its productions when justified. These restrictions may indicate the type of activity and specific audience limitations.

4-17. According to DA Pam 25-91, VI production supports DOD and the Joint Interest Program. Identify requirements at any level (installation, ASCC or field operating agency, HQDA) as having joint interest potential. Submit the production requirements to Army VI Management Office for validation.

4-18. The Army VI Management Office processes a non-validated requirement as an Army requirement. The Director, DIMOC on a case-by-case basis authorizes local replication by an authorized VI activity. Local authorization limits requests to those determined to be cost effective, time dependent, and in the best interest of the customer, requester, and the United States Army. When additional copies of a production are no longer required, the local authorized VI activity and specific audience limitations report to the DIMOC the number of copies removed from the activity inventory.

4-19. The VI manager at each level ensures that a distribution plan is prepared for all productions. The distribution plan includes the total number of copies required by the requester, the distribution format(s) and the proposed distribution of each copy to end users for extended loan through their servicing VI activity or directly to the VI libraries.

4-20. Forward obsolete VI productions distributed by the DIMOC to the United States Army VI Center that is no longer required for loan by the VI activity. The United States Army VI Center returns the VI productions to the DIMOC for reuse or disposition. The DIMOC may grant VI activities the authority to dispose of obsolete productions locally.

PHOTOGRAPHS

4-21. Photography uses wide shots, medium shots, and close-ups to capture a moment in time and space. Sequencing photographic moments in nearly the same manner videographers use scenes to tell a complete story. Photographs capture critical images such as terrain features, tactical deployments, intelligence information, and tactical operations. Photographs provide the operational commander through the President and Secretary of Defense a resource to enhance critical and timely operational decisions.

MULTIMEDIA PRESENTATIONS

4-22. Multimedia describes the ability to combine audio, video, and other information with graphics, control, storage, and other features of computer-based systems in the communication of information. The combination of several media often provides a richer, more effective flow of information or ideas than a single media, such as traditional text-based communications. Typically, recording multimedia presentations occurs continuously onto a motion medium, for replication or time-delayed playback, or for presentation in real time.

4-23. Multimedia products support a variety of purposes, from meeting training requirements to serving as a means to transmit public information. Multimedia products allow commanders to review the operations and training of their forces, and introduce new and improved operational techniques and developments to subordinates.

4-24. The intended audience determines the amount of editing time for a particular product. This results in a range of quality in multimedia products. The levels of editing are—

- **Rough edit video report productions** are normally products used by commanders and staffs at a local level to support their operational needs and are not viewed at higher levels.
- **Fully edited video productions** are normally products used by the theater command, joint headquarters, DOD, Joint Chiefs of Staff, or the President and Secretary of Defense to support operational needs.

4-25. VI productions are the results of sequencing, according to a plan or script, original or existing still, or motion images into a self-contained, complete, linear presentation for conveying information to or communicating with an audience. The inclusion of a scripted audio aspect defines a VI production specifically as an audiovisual production. Figure 4-3 documents an example of a linear presentation.

Figure 4-3. Linear presentation

AUDIO VIDEO PRODUCTION

4-26. Audio documentation can accompany video documentation, complement still slide shows, or stand alone, depending on the purpose of the presentation. Audio video production is VI production that combines motion media with sound.

GRAPHICS

4-27. Graphics are the product of designing, creating, and preparing two- and three-dimensional visual products manually, by machine or by computer. This capability can produce accurate and informative operational decision graphics or enhance maps, aerial photographs, and satellite imagery. Graphics creates overlays to emphasize or illustrate terrain and friendly, enemy, and targeting positions. Graphics incorporate visual imagery into maneuver control systems to enhance accurate representation of the operational environment. Graphics support preparing charts, posters, and visual materials for brochures, publication covers, briefings, displays, and models, as well as rough sketches and paintings for operational and historical purposes.

Chapter 5

Personnel Training

Visual information training prepares Soldiers to provide visual information support to commanders and their staffs. This chapter outlines the military occupational specialty training and the specialized training associated with visual information operations personnel.

VISUAL INFORMATION MILITARY OCCUPATIONAL SPECIALTIES

5-1. VI operations require highly trained VI Soldiers that can deploy to austere environments at a moment's notice to support VI missions. The following paragraphs discuss the four military occupational specialties (MOS) in the Career Management Field 25 responsible for accomplishing the VI mission.

MULTIMEDIA ILLUSTRATOR

5-2. The Army produces training manuals, newspapers, reports, and promotional materials on a regular basis. As an integral member of the Army's multimedia team, the Multimedia Illustrator (MOS 25M) produces graphic artwork, drawings, and other visual displays. Graphic artwork product support includes publications, signs, charts, posters, television, and motion picture productions. Some of the duties of a multimedia illustrator may include—

- Supervising, planning, and operating manual, mechanical, and electric multimedia imaging equipment to produce various kinds of visual displays and documents.
- Creating illustrations, layouts, map overlays, posters, graphs, and charts to support Army combat and non-combat operations.
- Producing computer-generated graphics.
- Drawing graphs and charts to represent budgets, numbers of Soldiers, supply levels and office organization.
- Drawing caricatures for filmstrips and creating animation for films.
- Working with television and film producers to design backdrops and props for film sets.
- Installing, operating, and performing maintenance on equipment.
- Performing preventive maintenance checks and services (PMCS) on vehicles and generators.

5-3. The multimedia illustrator operates the following equipment—

- Graphics computers.
- Headliners.
- Video projectors.
- Photo composers.
- Desktop publishing equipment.
- Digital information handlers.
- Still photography editing and processing systems.

VISUAL INFORMATION EQUIPMENT OPERATOR MAINTAINER

5-4. Although the Army does not produce box office movies, television and film productions are still an important part of Army communications. VI Equipment Operator Maintainer (MOS 25R) is primarily responsible for supporting Army operations with VI equipment and systems. VI equipment operator maintainer, perform many specialized tasks, ranging from maintaining forms, records, to operating audio recording devices, and maintaining VI equipment and systems. Some of the duties of a VI equipment operator maintainer may include—

- Operating and performing maintenance on television receivers, monitors, and cameras.
- Working with computer controlled video switchers, audio mixers, and consoles.
- Working with synchronous generators, distribution equipment and amplifying equipment.
- Operating and performing maintenance on motion and still photo imaging equipment, closed circuit systems, visual imagery satellite, microwave, radio frequency transmission, and cable distribution systems.
- Operating media equipment and special effect devices including cameras, sound recorders and lighting.

5-5. The VI equipment operator maintainer is also responsible for—

- Installing, operating, maintaining, and performing unit and higher levels of maintenance on VI equipment and systems to support Army, joint, and multinational operations.
- Operating vehicles and maintaining forms, records, repair parts, special tools, and test equipment.
- Installing, operating, and performing unit and direct support maintenance on equipment and performs PMCS on vehicles and generators.

5-6. The VI equipment operator maintainer operates and maintains the following equipment—

- Army inventory and commercial television and radio broadcasting systems and associated equipment.
- Desktop publishing equipment.
- Electronic still photography systems.
- Still photography editing and processing systems.
- Motion video acquisition systems.
- Motion video editing systems.
- VI satellite support equipment.

COMBAT DOCUMENTATION PRODUCTION SPECIALIST

5-7. Combat Documentation Production Specialists (MOS 25V), are primarily responsible for supervising, planning, operating electronic and film-based still video, and audio acquisition equipment to document combat and non-combat operations. Some of the duties of a combat documentation production specialist may include—

- Operating broadcast, collection, and television production and distribution equipment.
- Creating VI products to support combat documentation, MISO, military intelligence, medical, public affairs, training, and other functions.
- Performing operator maintenance on motion, still and studio television cameras.
- Preparing captions for documentation images.
- Working with writers, producers, and directors in preparing and interpreting scripts.
- Planning and designing production scenery, graphics, and special effects.
- Operating media equipment and special effect devices, including cameras, sound recorders and lighting.
- Following script and instructions of film or television directors to move cameras, zoom, pan or adjust focus.
- Capture, edit, and transmit tactical digital media with a high degree of accuracy to support the commander's themes and messages.

5-8. The combat documentation production specialist operates the following equipment—

- Commercial still and video camera systems.
- Other Army inventory and commercial processing and finishing equipment.

- Non-developmental item digital acquisition equipment.
- Electronic still photography systems.
- Still photography editing and processing systems.
- Motion video acquisition systems.
- Motion video editing systems.
- VI satellite support equipment.

VISUAL INFORMATION OPERATIONS CHIEF

5-9.   The VI Operations Chief (MOS 25Z) can operate all major equipment used by the multimedia illustrator, VI equipment operator maintainer, and combat documentation production specialist. The VI operations chief has the following responsibilities and duties—

- Plans, programs, and supervises personnel performing VI support for Army, joint, and multinational operations.
- Manages visual information documentation production schedules, multimedia illustration, television productions, and VI equipment repair operations and facilities.
- Supervises combat documentation, MISO, military intelligence, training, and special functions.
- Plans, coordinates, and supervises activities pertaining to organization, training, and combat operations.
- Edits and prepares tactical plans and training material.
- Coordinates implementation of operations, training programs, and communications activities.
- Establishes equipment maintenance and production schedules.
- Supervises installation, operation, and maintenance of equipment.
- Supervises PMCS on vehicles and generators.

VISUAL INFORMATION SPECIALIZED TRAINING

5-10.   VI personnel receive specialized training (advanced field training and weapons qualifications) allowing the personnel to integrate with any combat unit in austere and hostile environments. VI personnel also obtain other specific qualifications to document specialized operations of any type, such as divers; airborne, fixed, and rotary wing aircrew; visit, board, search and seizure, and maritime security operations; fast rope procedures; rappelling; and other specialized combat skills. The following paragraphs discuss the training relative to VI personnel.

UNITED STATES ARMY CYBER CENTER OF EXCELLENCE

5-11.   The Commanding General, Cyber Center of Excellence, directs and supervises all officer and enlisted service school training for Career Management Field 25 and VI MOSs. A majority of the resident training to support the VI mission occurs at the Defense Information School, Fort Meade, Maryland. The senior enlisted advisor for Career Management Field 25 series MOS works in the Office of the Chief of Signal, Cyber Center of Excellence.

DEFENSE INFORMATION SCHOOL

5-12.   The Defense Information School (DINFOS) provides resident, entry-level, and advanced training in public affairs, journalism, photojournalism, broadcasting, graphics, electronic imaging, broadcast systems maintenance, video production, and VI management. The DINFOS provides officers, enlisted personnel, and civilian employees of all branches of the Armed forces with the required training to prepare them for worldwide assignments throughout the DOD.

5-13.   The DINFOS VI course work covers the following topics—

- Electronic imaging.
- Imagery systems maintenance.
- Broadcast television systems maintenance.

- Graphics.
- Still photography.
- Television equipment maintenance.
- Electronic fundamentals.
- Photographic maintenance.
- Photographic processing maintenance.
- Quality control.
- VI management.
- Themes and messages.

5-14. The following paragraphs discuss the training performed at the DINFOS.

Basic Multimedia Illustrator Course

5-15. The Basic Multimedia Illustrator Course provides MOS 25M students with the skills required to perform the duties and fulfill the responsibilities required in the combat field graphics and graphics designer career field. Training includes classes in the principles of design and layout, fundamentals of color theory, drawing, color media, perspective, typography, printing, electronic imaging systems, graphic design, image editing, desktop publishing, multimedia, and telecommunications software. Students learn the operational principles of image scanners, digitizing devices, output to black and white and color printers, film and video recorders, plotters, image and data transmission, archiving data and image files, along with computer management principles and operator maintenance. Students participate in classes on VI ethics, visual communications, and customer relations.

Basic Still Photography Course

5-16. The Basic Still Photography Course is a prerequisite course for attendance at the Video Production and Documentation Course before award of MOS 25V. The course provides class instruction and practical exercises in theory and application of photographic fundamentals, captioning, optics, light sources, camera operations for standard and studio photography, electronic flash, automatic paper processors, and picture story. Students also become skilled at using electronic imaging systems including digital cameras and imaging and graphic software. Students are introduced to combat documentation and field imagery transmission, editing, and archiving digital images depicting all aspects of the United States military, including military operations, exercises, training and military life. Upon completion of this course, Army students must follow on to the Video Production and Documentation Course.

Video Production and Documentation Course

5-17. The Video Production and Documentation Course is the follow on course to the Basic Still Photography Course and after successful completion, Soldiers are awarded MOS 25V. The course provides training on the principles, techniques, and skills required to perform the duties and functions of production and combat documentation specialists. This course also provides training in the knowledge and skills needed to perform the duties required for VI production assignments supporting video documentation of training and operations, public affairs, joint operations, and studio missions throughout the Armed Forces. The scope of training includes the operation of the digital video camera, lighting equipment, the principles of framing and composition, camera placement, audio and video editing, visualization, storytelling, and a working knowledge of audio and video applications for television electronic field production and studio operations.

Intermediate Videography Course

5-18. The Intermediate Videography Course students focus on learning and practicing the intermediate skills necessary to perform proficiently at a journeyman level of video storytelling and production. This course reinforces skills and expands the concepts of narrative and non-narrative productions. This course introduces the advanced techniques used in these productions with emphasis on advanced non-linear editing techniques. Each student learns and practices the role and responsibilities of performing as a team leader. The Intermediate Videography Course is open to E-4 through E-6 25V, or E-7 25Z personnel with one year experience that have graduated from the Video Production and Documentation Course.

Digital Multimedia Course

5-19. The Digital Multimedia Course provides intermediate level training in the knowledge and skills needed to create and integrate text, graphics, sound, animation, and full-motion video into multimedia and web-based packages. The course includes instruction in the operation of computer systems, input devices and output devices to acquire, edit, design, manage, output, and archive digital imaging, graphic design and multimedia files. Students use software to create, manage, and render the following: composite photographic layouts, graphic designs, page layouts, video productions, web pages, and interactive multimedia solutions. The course also includes theoretical and working instruction of computer fundamentals and functions, communications, color theory, and the principles and implementation of color management. The course also emphasizes DOD policies and instructions relative to ethics and use of computer generated and edited images.

5-20. The Digital Multimedia Course is open to the following military and civilian personnel that have a fundamental knowledge of, and currently involved in daily VI operations—

* Enlisted: E-4 through E-7 (25M, 25V, 25Z).
* Civilians: GS-07 through GS-11 (Series 1001, 1020, 1035, 1060, 1071, 1084).

5-21. A fundamental knowledge requires two years of computer experience in the last five years, including operational skills in the following types of software: raster-based, vector-based, and digital page layout. Experience using these fundamental skills is necessary to prepare students for this fast-paced, intermediate level course. The Registrar and Quota Management Office verify that students meet prerequisites via a Digital Multimedia Course Prerequisite Verification Letter. The verification letter is required to complete registration. Prerequisites for the Digital Multimedia Course are non-waiverable, and require verification and approval to confirm a reservation in the course.

Visual Information Management Course

5-22. The VI Management Course provides in-depth training in the duties required to manage VI operations. This course is in resident only at the DINFOS. Students apply doctrine and policy during seminars and practical exercises to the management of VI operations. The course covers the following subjects—

* Overview of VI in the Department of Defense including policy, doctrine, and ethics.
* VI production process.
* The budgeting process.
* VI support for contingencies, joint operations, IO, and combat camera operations.

5-23. Army personnel that attend the VI Management Course must meet the following prerequisites—

* Enlisted: E-7 through E-9 25Z.
* Officer: O-2 through O-4.
* Civilian: GS-09 through GS-13 (10XX series).

Visual Information Operator Maintainer

5-24. The VI Operator Maintainer Course trains MOS 25R Soldiers to install, operate, maintain, and perform unit and higher levels of maintenance on VI equipment and systems. Advanced Individual Training provides Soldiers training on maintaining forms, records, prescribed load lists, the use of special tools and test equipment; and training on performing PMCS on vehicles and generators.

COMCAM Leadership Course

5-25. The COMCAM Leadership Course trains selected officers and senior NCOs in the principles, techniques, and skills required to perform the duties and functions of a COMCAM officer and COMCAM NCO in charge. The course focuses on identifying the mission and functions of COMCAM including the development of operational support plans, budgets, equipment systems maintenance plans, centralized supply management, policy and procedures, marketing plans, imagery management plans, and training plans. The course also includes in-depth theoretical and working knowledge of how COMCAM functions in the DOD. The prerequisites for this course are—

- Officers O-1 through O-4 assigned to a COMCAM unit.
- 25Z on assignment to or at the 55th Signal Company or 982nd Signal Company.
- With waiver E-6, 25V, 25M, 25R in a leadership position.
- Hold a SECRET security clearance.

Signal Corps Regimental Noncommissioned Officer Academy Detachment

5-26. The Signal Corps Regimental NCO Academy Detachment is a subordinate element of the Signal Corps Regimental NCO Academy at Fort Gordon, Georgia. The Signal Corps Regimental NCO Academy Detachment provides resident Advanced Leaders Course and Senior Leaders Course at Fort Meade, Maryland. NCOs in the ranks of sergeant (promotable), staff sergeant, and sergeant first class from Career Management Fields 25 receive training at the academy under the NCO Education System.

5-27. The Advanced Leaders Course teaches common leader combat skills, as well as technical excellence in VI operations. The course emphasizes planning, leading, and directing the operations of Combat Documentation and Production Specialists (25V), Multimedia Illustrators (25M), and VI Equipment Operators and Maintainers (25R). The Signal Corps Regimental NCO Academy Detachment also teaches the VI Operations Chief Senior Leaders Course (25Z).

OTHER SPECIALIZED TRAINING

5-28. The unit commander identifies and programs other specialized training such as airborne training to fulfill a unit's mission. The requirements for other specialized training require documenting on the unit's table of organization and equipment or Tables of Distribution and Allowance.

442d SIGNAL BATTALION

5-29. The 442d Signal Battalion trains Signal Regiment officers (first lieutenant through captain) developing the officers with the necessary leadership, technical and tactical skills to support Army and joint forces. The courses trained by the 442d Signal Battalion are—

- Signal Basic Officer Leader Course Phase III:
  - Provides Signal officers training on communications planning and management; communications interface; leadership; IT; electronics; microwave; tropospheric scattering; property accounting; telecommunications; communications security accounting; management of training; military justice; signal systems tactics and doctrine.
  - The course also includes communications requirements, planning and execution specific to a movement battalion or maneuver enhancement brigade.
- Signal Captains Career Course for Regular Army:
  - Provides Regular Army Signal officers the academic instruction, which supports the leader, tactical, and technical skills needed to lead company-size units and to serve at battalion and brigade level staffs.
  - The course is a twenty-week residency course.
- Signal Captains Career Course for Army Reserve provides the Army Reserve Signal officer academic instruction using a four-phase process. Army Reserve Signal officers conduct phase one and three through distance learning, and phase two and four in residency. The course provides Army Reserve Signal officers with technical updates related to:
  - Communications interfaces.
  - Electronic warfare.
  - Chemical, biological, radiological, and nuclear operations.
  - Leadership.

- Human resources support.
- Property accounting.
- Training management.
- Force integration.
- Military justice.
- Signal system tactics and doctrine.

5-30. The mission of the 442d Signal Battalion is to prepare Signal Corps company grade Regular Army and Army Reserve officers for company level command, and for assignments to staff positions at battalions and brigades, both Signal and Non-Signal, with a primary emphasis on signal operations.

5-31. The 442d Signal Battalion is part of the Leader College of Information Technology at Cyber Center of Excellence and information on Signal officer education and training can be obtained by contacting the Chief, Officer Education and Training Division.

5-32. Personnel interested in attending a 442d Signal Battalion or NCO Academy Course should contact their branch or functional area representative, local post or installation training coordinator for Army Training Resources and Requirements System enrollment or the 442d Signal Battalion, Training Support Division.

ON-THE-JOB TRAINING

5-33. Formal school training supplemented by on-the-job training improves individual proficiency and builds teamwork. On-the-job training and cross training of VI Soldiers is a command responsibility. Cross training provides for continuity throughout the organization.

UNIT TRAINING

5-34. Leaders in VI units are responsible for planning training that guarantees a high standard of wartime proficiency. Training should focus on image acquisition, processing, reproducing, and distribution in a tactical operations environment, the effective use of available time and resources, and the maintenance of all equipment.

ARMY CORRESPONDENCE COURSE PROGRAM

5-35. The Army Correspondence Course Program offers nonresident VI training. The Cyber Center of Excellence determines VI correspondence course offerings and eligibility. However, the Army Institute for Professional Development, United States Army Training Support Center, Fort Eustis, Virginia, administers the program.

5-36. The Army Correspondence Course Program offers both individual and group study enrollment options. With individual study, the student decides on course work to pursue and the timetable for completing it. With group study, a group leader administers the course to a group of students. Group study can be an effective way to conduct additional unit training, especially in low-density MOS situations.

5-37. The Army Training Support Center governs the policies and procedures for enrolling in Army correspondence courses. The list of all correspondence courses developed and administered by the Army as well as enrollment, courseware content, and examinations can be accessed by logging onto the Army Training (and Education) Network website. Address questions concerning enrollment eligibility waivers for current course configurations or problems with VI sub courses to the United States Army Signal School Detachment.

This page intentionally left blank.

Chapter 6

Life Cycle Sustainment

Visual information equipment and systems require sustainment over the equipment and systems life cycle. This chapter addresses life cycle sustainment relative to visual information equipment and systems, equipment planning, capability developers, materiel developers, supplies and repair parts, and maintenance.

VISUAL INFORMATION EQUIPMENT AND SYSTEMS

6-1. According to with Department of Defense Instruction 5000.02, *Operation of the Defense Acquisition System*, life cycle sustainment translates force provider capability and performance requirements into tailored product support to achieve specified and evolving life-cycle product support availability, reliability, and affordability parameters. VI equipment and systems are items of a nonexpendable or durable nature capable of continuous or repetitive use. VI production items consist of items used for recording, producing, reproducing, processing, broadcasting, editing, distributing, exhibiting, and storing VI products. A VI system exists when a number of interconnected VI components operate together as designed. When items that could otherwise be called non-VI equipment are an integral part of a VI system (existing or under development), sustain the items as part of that VI system.

6-2. VI activities are authorized equipment and systems to produce products and provide services at their approved capability levels. VI COTS investment items are DA controlled with a cost threshold established by Congress. The requesting field operating agency VI manager in coordination with the Network Enterprise Center validates VI systems and equipment requirements costing in excess of the established threshold before forwarding to HQDA, CIO/G-6. The Army CIO/G-6 oversees the Army information resource management process and manages resources to prioritize and fund VI systems and equipment using Management Decision Packages. The Television-Audio Support Activity an organization under Defense Media Activity's Technical Services Directorate is the item commodity managers for the acquisition of commercial VI equipment, systems, and supplies. The Television-Audio Support Activity procures nontactical VI equipment and systems costing $50,000 or more. Installations and field operating agency VI managers may provide supplemental investment funds for the acquisition of CIO/G-6-approved requirements. Procurement of expense items for equipment that costs less than $50,000 occurs locally upon approval of the Network Enterprise Center.

VISUAL INFORMATION EQUIPMENT PLANNING

6-3. VI managers plan for VI equipment to meet their current and projected needs per the Army VI strategy. Each VI manager develops and forwards requirements for investment equipment using a consolidated six-year plan. This plan is the basis for establishing annual funding increments for equipment replacement. VI managers also submit investment VI equipment requirements for inclusion in the Program Objective Memorandum submissions. VI activity managers plan for VI expense and investment equipment through installation resource management channels as part of their annual operating budget.

6-4. Commands with authorized VI activities establish and maintain a five-year VI requirements plan for equipment to meet their current and projected acquisition needs. This plan establishes an annual, realistic basis for programming both new and replacement equipment requirements. DA Pam 25-91 contains sample plans.

6-5. A VI activity assigned a new mission requirement can use the new requirement to justify planning for and the purchase of new VI equipment. The Army VI Management Office must approve the expanded capability.

6-6. Replacement equipment requirements entail planning and programming based on the life expectancy of equipment currently installed or in use. This provides a basis for establishing annual funding increments for replacing equipment. Table 6-1 is a guide to help in determining the life expectancy of VI equipment.

Table 6-1. A guide to the life expectancy of VI equipment

Type of equipment	Installation	Life expectancy years
Photographic systems		
All still and motion picture cameras (except self-processing cameras)	Transportable	6
	Portable	5
Self-processing cameras	Transportable	5
	Portable	5
Ancillary motion picture equipment: film editing, splicing, sound readers, synchronizers, and similar equipment	Fixed	10
Presentation equipment: all types of projectors, screens, and accessory equipment	Transportable	10
Audio systems		
Audio amplification equipment: audio tape recorders and players, disc players, public address systems, and accessory equipment	Fixed	7
	Transportable	5
	Portable	5
Audio microphone, mixing and control equipment, distribution equipment, speakers, and recorders	Fixed	7
	Transportable	5
	Portable	5
Video systems		
Video camera systems, synchronization generation, and switching	Fixed	6
	Transportable	5
	Portable	5
Video editing systems and character generators	Fixed	5
	Transportable	5
	Portable	5
Studio equipment: lighting, dollies, pedestals, tripods, booms, prompting equipment, and associated gear	Fixed	10
	Transportable	5
Still video and still store frame systems	Fixed	5
	Transportable	5
Ancillary technical plant equipment	Fixed	10
Film chains	Fixed	6
Closed circuit television systems	Fixed	10
Graphic arts equipment		
Computer graphics equipment	Fixed	5
Composing machines, typesetters, and title making machines	Fixed	5
Vapor process printers, art projector viewers, fluorescent tracing boxes, drafting tables, and dry mount presses	Fixed	10
Tactical Digital Media Kits	Transportable fly away	3 years

6-7. The procuring activity for VI equipment provides the logistic supportability of COTS materiel. The local signal supporting activity coordinates local procurement to consolidate maintenance service contracts.

The Army must certify VI equipment and systems with network or wireless interface capability as DOD IT Standards Registry compliant before acquisition.

VISUAL INFORMATION CAPABILITY DEVELOPERS

6-8. VI capability developers provide the doctrine, materiel requirements, organizations, and management information systems for new concepts. They have the following responsibilities—

- Determine the maintenance impact resulting from new ideas or materiel solutions.
- Help in planning for logistics demonstrations and maintenance tests and analyze the results.
- Resolve issues relating to reliability, availability, maintainability, and supportability.
- Determine requirements and develop the documentation for training devices.
- Develop techniques, determine skill requirements for battle damage assessment, and repair.
- Coordinate with materiel developers to ensure materiel maintenance considerations are included in the requirements documents.

6-9. The Cyber Center of Excellence, United States Army Training and Doctrine Command, provides the capability development for tactical VI systems. The Cyber Center of Excellence develops, plans, and coordinates concepts for tactical VI organizations; VI equipment systems, and prepares the table of organization and equipment force requirements within the force structure.

6-10. The appropriate authorization document table of organization and equipment and modified table of organization and equipment include the approved requirements. Tactical VI organizations with an approved unit identification code maintain a centralized listing of tactical VI equipment and systems.

VISUAL INFORMATION MATERIEL DEVELOPERS

6-11. VI Materiel Developers have the following responsibilities—

- Ensure the fielding plan meets the requirements of Army maintenance systems, and that reliability, availability, and maintainability are included in design parameters and demonstrated during operational testing.
- Participate in the planning and execution of logistics demonstrations and operational maintenance testing.
- Ensure trained personnel, test measurement and diagnostic equipment, facilities, support equipment, repair parts, and publications are available after system delivery to the user.
- Establish and monitor modification work order programs.
- Develop battle damage assessment and repair techniques, procedures, and related tool and materiel requirements.
- Develop factors for determining operational readiness float requirements, and submit the factors to HQDA for approval.
- Emphasize prognostics and diagnostics in the design, development, and improvement of equipment.
- Collect data from all maintenance levels to analyze and use for prognostic purposes.

6-12. The materiel developers establish annual review procedures to ensure tactical VI equipment and repair part allowances and inventories are valid. Obsolete or underused equipment and parts require redistribution for disposal.

VISUAL INFORMATION SUPPLIES AND REPAIR PARTS

6-13. Standard equipment, when authorized requires requisitioning through the Army Wholesale Supply System. Tactical digital media organizations with an approved table of organization and equipment and modified table of organization and equipment authorization use type classified standard equipment, when possible.

6-14. The Army Wholesale Supply System supports repair parts for approved VI equipment and systems. When equipment in the Wholesale Supply System does not meet the operational requirements, the Material Developer initiates a product improvement plan.

VISUAL INFORMATION MAINTENANCE

6-15. VI operators and maintainers perform preventive maintenance on VI equipment according to the manufacturers' prescribed scheduled maintenance. VI operators and maintainers manage VI equipment according to AR 750-1. The maintenance policy is—

- Develop and field a maintenance plan with the materiel as part of the logistic support. COTS materiel procurement includes the equivalent of a maintenance support plan or justification for contract maintenance or inter-service support.
- Maintain training circular VI materiel per the maintenance allocation chart. Refer support requirements beyond the user's authority and all non-training circular audiovisual materiel to the common support VI activity or the Network Enterprise Center.
- The training community may, at the option of the Army command, ASCC, and direct reporting unit, manage maintenance of VI equipment and activities integrated with training device support activities. Otherwise, submit contract requirements to the supporting Network Enterprise Center, who coordinates the support.
- User commands are responsible for contract maintenance support and budgeting funds for all VI materiel under their control. The user commands provide funds to the supporting Network Enterprise Center or VI activity to support contract efforts.

6-16. The Television-Audio Support Activity provides life cycle sustainment support for broadcast and VI equipment. The VI activity maintains and repairs installed or fixed VI equipment after any warranties have expired The forms required for sustainment support are:

- DA Form 5988-E (Equipment Inspection Maintenance Worksheet) or DA Form 2404 (Equipment Inspection and Maintenance Worksheet).
- DA Form 5990-E (Maintenance Request).

Glossary

The glossary lists acronyms and terms with Army, multi-service, or joint definitions, and other selected terms. Where Army and joint definitions are different, (Army) follows the term. Terms for which ATP 6-02.40 is the proponent manual (the authority) are marked with an asterisk (*). The proponent manual for other terms is listed in parentheses after the definition.

SECTION I – ACRONYMS AND ABBREVIATIONS

AR	Army regulation
ASCC	Army Service component command
ATP	Army techniques publication
COMCAM	combat camera
CIO	chief information officer
COTS	commercial off-the-shelf
DA	Department of the Army
DA Pam	Department of the Army pamphlet
DIMOC	Defense Imagery Management Operations Center
DINFOS	Defense Information School
DOD	Department of Defense
FM	field manual
FORSCOM	United States Army Forces Command
HQDA	Headquarters, Department of the Army
IO	information operations
IT	information technology
J-39	Joint Staff, Deputy Director for Global Operations
MISO	military information support operations
MOS	military occupational specialty
NCO	noncommissioned officer
PMCS	preventive maintenance checks and service
VI	visual information

SECTION II – TERMS

accessioning

(DOD) The acts and procedures by which records are taken into the physical custody of a record holdings activity, archival agency, or other record repository. (DODI 5040.02)

acquisition

(DOD) In VI, the process of recording VI in a camera; creating it by hand, mechanically, or on a computer; or obtaining it by purchase, donation, or seizure. (DODI 5040.02)

archival master

(DOD) VI media, designated as an archival master by the DIMOC, that either consists of the Camera original or contains one or more VI records copied from the camera original media or file (or the best available copy) to best preserve VI content. (DODI 5040.02)

broadcast

(Army) The transmission of radio, television, and data signals through the air waves or fiber optic cable. (AR 25-1)

caption

(DOD) Short explanatory or descriptive data accompanying imagery. A caption should answer who, what, when, where, how, how many, and why questions relative to the imagery. Captions are embedded as metadata in digital imagery. (DODI 5040.02)

captions

(DOD) Display of spoken dialogue as printed words on a television, computer, projection, or other type of screen. Unlike subtitles, captions are specifically designed for hearing impaired viewers. They may include information regarding on- and off-screen sound effects, such as music or laughter. Captions come in two forms: open and closed. Open captions are displayed automatically as part of the video, without selection by the user. Closed captions normally do not appear unless the user has selected them to appear. (DODI 5040.07)

clearance for public release

(DOD) The determination by responsible officials that a DOD production and the information contained therein are not classified; do not conflict with established DOD or Federal Government policies or programs; and comply with applicable laws and regulations, and, therefore, are releasable to the public. (DODI 5040.07)

combat camera

(DOD) The acquisition and use of still and motion imagery in support of combat, information, humanitarian, special force, intelligence, reconnaissance, engineering, legal, public affairs, and other operations involving the Military Services by COMCAM forces specifically trained, organized, equipped, and tasked to provide such support. (DODI 5040.02)

Defense Imagery Management Operations Center

(DOD) The DOD's central VI enterprise level activity for collection, management, storage, and distribution of classified and unclassified strategic, operational, tactical, and joint-interest still and motion imagery, VI end products and records. (DODI 5040.02)

Defense Visual Information Activity Number

(DOD) A unique identifier assigned to each authorized DOD VI activity. (DODI 5040.07)

distribution

(DOD) In VI, the process of supplying an end product to its intended end users, by any means. (DODI 5040.02)

documentation imagery

(DOD) Imagery depicting actual events, activities, phenomena, places, or people recorded primarily to create a record of the subject matter. (DODI 5040.7)

graphic art

(DOD) In VI, hand-, mechanically-, or computer-drawn art works or pictorial representations that are created rather than recorded in a camera. (DODI 5040.02)

imagery

(DOD) A visual representation of a person, place, or thing recorded and stored in any format, in electronic or in a physical medium. (DODI 5040.02)

information technology

(Army) Any equipment or interconnected system or subsystem of equipment that is used in the automatic acquisition, storage, manipulation, management, movement, control, display, switching, interchange, transmission, or reception of data or information by the executive agency. For purposes of the preceding sentence, equipment is used by an executive agency if the equipment is used directly or is used by a contractor under a contract with the executive agency, which 1) requires the use of such equipment; or 2) requires the use, to a significant extent, of such equipment in the performance of a service or the furnishing of a product. The term "information technology" also includes computers, ancillary equipment, software, firmware, and similar procedures, services (including support services), and related resources. The term "information technology" does not include any equipment that is acquired by a Federal contractor incidental to a Federal contract. (Reference 40 USC Subtitle III (Clinger-Cohen Act of 1996).) (AR 25-1)

life cycle

(Army) The total phases that an item progresses through from the time it is initially developed until the time it is either consumed, in use, or disposed of as being excess. (AR 25-1)

media

(DOD) Any films, videotapes, discs, or other physical objects that contain or are capable of containing visual information. (DOD 5040.6-M-2)

video

(DOD) Motion imagery that is recorded or transmitted as either a digital or analog electromagnetic signal. (DODI 5040.02)

visual information

(DOD) Various visual media with or without sound. Generally, visual information includes still photography, motion picture photography, video or audio recording, graphic arts, visual aids, models, display, visual presentation. (DODI 5040.07)

visual information activity

(DOD) An organizational element or a function within an organization, whose principal responsibility is to provide VI products and/or services and which is assigned an authorizing DVIAN. (DODI 5040.07)

visual information documentation

(Army) Motion media, still photography, and audio recording of technical and nontechnical events, as they occur, and are usually not controlled by the recording crew. (AR 25-1)

visual information production

(Army) The combination of motion media with sound in a self-contained, complete presentation, developed according to a plan or script for purpose of conveying information to, or communicating with, an audience. A production is also the end item of the production process. Used collectively, VI production refers to the functions of procurement, production or adoption from all sources, such as in-house or contract production, off-the-shelf purchase, or adoption from another Federal agency. (AR 25-1)

visual information records

(Army) VI materials, regardless of format, and related captions and intellectual control data. (AR 25-1)

This page intentionally left blank.

References

REQUIRED PUBLICATIONS

These documents must be available to the intended users of this publication.

ADRP 1-02. *Terms and Military Symbols.* 24 September 2013.

JP 1-02. *Department of Defense Dictionary of Military and Associated Terms.* 08 November 2010.

RELATED PUBLICATIONS

These documents contain relevant supplemental information.

JOINT PUBLICATIONS

Most joint and Department of Defense doctrinal publications are available online:
http://www.dtic.mil/doctrine/new_pubs/jointpub.htm.

DOD 5040.6-M-2. *Instructions for Handling Visual Information (VI) Material.* 20 April 2005.

DODI 5000.02. *Operation of the Defense Acquisition System.* 25 November 2013.

DODI 5040.02. *Visual Information (VI).* 27 October 2011.

DODI 5040.07. *Visual Information (VI) Productions.* 21 February 2013.

DODI 5200.02. *DOD Personnel Security Program (PSP).* 21 March 2014.

DODM 5040.06. *Visual Information (VI), Volume 3, VI Records Schedule.* 25 September 2008.

ARMY PUBLICATIONS

Most Army doctrinal publications are available online: http://www.apd.army.mil/

ADP 1-02. *Operational Terms and Military Symbols.* 31 August 2012.

AR 25-1. *Army Information Technology.* 25 June 2013.

AR 25-400-2. *The Army Records Information Management System (ARIMS).* 2 October 2007.

AR 700-131. *Loan, Lease, and Donation of Army Materiel.* 23 August 2004.

AR 71-9. *Warfighting Capabilities Determination.* 28 December 2009.

AR 735-5. *Property Accountability Policies.* 10 May 2013.

AR 750-1. *Army Materiel Maintenance Policy.* 12 September 2013.

ATP 5-19. *Risk Management.* 14 April 2014.

DA Pam 25-91. *Visual Information Procedures.* 1 July 2014.

FM 6-02. *Signal Support to Operations.* 22 January 2014.

FM 27-10. *The Law of Land Warfare.* 18 July 1956.

OTHER PUBLICATIONS

Joint Visual Information Concept of Operations. 27 October 2011.

Joint Combat Camera Visual Information Smart Book. 2013 Edition.

PRESCRIBED FORMS

None

REFERENCED FORMS

Unless otherwise indicated, DA Forms are available on the Army Publishing Directorate (APD) website: www.apd.army.mil.

DA Form 2028. *Recommended Changes to Publications and Blank Forms.*

DA Form 2404. *Equipment Inspection and Maintenance Worksheet.*

DA Form 5988-E. *Equipment Inspection Maintenance Worksheet.*

DA Form 5990-E. *Maintenance Request.*

DD Form 1995. *Visual Information (VI) Production Request and Report.*

DD Form 2537. *Visual Information Caption Sheet.*

DD Form 2858. *Visual Information Activity Profile.*

DD Forms are available on the Office of the Secretary of Defense (OSD) web site:
http://www.dtic.mil/whs/directives/infomgt/forms/.

WEBSITES

APD Web site is www.apd.army.mil

Defense Imagery Web site is http://www.defenseimagery.mil.

Doctrinal Terminology & Symbology Group https://www.milsuite.mil/book/groups/army-marine-corps-terminology.

Joint Doctrine, Education, and Training Electronic Information System Web site https://jdeis.js.mil/jdeis/index.jsp?pindex=0.

Joint Electronic Library http://www.dtic.mil/doctrine/new_pubs/jointpub.htm.

U.S. Defense Information School http://www.dinfos.dma.mil

Index

ATP 6-20.40 (FM 6-20.40)
27 October 2014

By Order of the Secretary of the Army

RAYMOND T. ODIERNO
General, United States Army
Chief of Staff

Official:

GERALD B. O'KEEFE
Administrative Assistant to the
Secretary of the Army
1428103